# Pollution:
# The Effluence of Affluence

# Pollution:
# The Effluence of Affluence

## Selected Readings

Edited by

**Frank J. Taylor**
**Philip G. Kettle**
**Robert G. Putnam**

# Methuen

Toronto    London    Sydney    Wellington

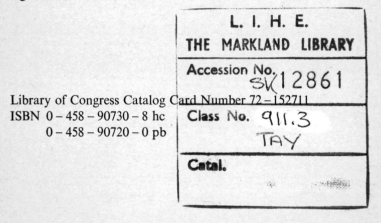

Library of Congress Catalog Card Number 72 – 152711
ISBN  0 – 458 – 90730 – 8 hc
      0 – 458 – 90720 – 0 pb

The text of this book was typeset and printed by The Bryant Press
Limited, Toronto.

Text type is Monotype 10 on 12 Times Roman on a twenty-five pica measure.
Headings are set in various sizes of Univers Bold.

The text was printed by offset lithography on 60 lb. Cartier Litho by a
sheet-fed Harris offset.

Binding and cover printing were done by The Bryant Press Limited, Toronto.

Artwork by Antony Bradshaw.

74  73  72  71  1  2  3  4  5

# Contents

A complete list of contents will be found at the beginning of each section.

v

# Photographs

The Publishers acknowledge permission to reproduce photographs from the following sources:

British Columbia Government Photograph    Page 180

Communicate Limited    Page 169

Ontario Department of Energy and Resources Management    Page 144

Ontario Department of Lands and Forests    Page 181

Ontario Water Resources Commission    Pages 79, 96, 99, 103, 121, 131, 139, 193, 194

Miller Services    Pages 72, 74, 156, 161

Toronto Star Syndicate    Pages 67, 76, 77, 86, 87, 119, 146, 173

Toronto Telegram Syndicate    Pages 47, 94

# Preface

Most of us will agree that pollution is undesirable. The degree and range of undesirability is perhaps determined by the extent to which each individual is exposed to pollution, and in what form. The urban dweller chokes through the haze that enshrouds his city. The near-airport resident is battered by noise from jet aircraft. The cottager recoils from algae-stricken and oil-slicked lakes. The lover of the countryside finds his view of nature obscured by that prolific sub-species, *Canus stannis*, and its recent mutation, *Botulis nonreturnibilis*. The fisherman finds that pesticide control does not stop with the shore.

Surely the solution is easy. We simply stop polluting – and everyone benefits. But the automobile that smogs our cities also carries us to our lake retreat or ski lodge. The generating plant lights our houses and powers our television sets. The pesticide that kills our birdlife enables us to eat worm-free apples. In short, almost all forms of pollution result from some process or action that we, as individuals or a society, consider desirable or necessary.

This, then, is the dilemma. Pollution is undesirable, but the activities that cause it are not. Is there a solution? Are we doomed to burn up the life support systems of our multi-million ton space capsule?

From scholarly writings, and from the news media, the editors have selected a group of articles, opinions, and comments on pollution. This material attempts to show how controversial and widespread the pollution question has become. In certain areas, some answers and solutions seem to be available – even obvious. In other areas, however, the dilemma is very real. The reader is urged to investigate further the problems that threaten all of us.

From the mass of information and opinion, one point of view seems to provide a starting place for considering solutions. The earth is a closed system. Its only input is energy from the sun, and that supply is constant. Certain resources are non-renewable – minerals, for example. These are finite, and will be used up – some are close to that point already. Others, such as water and oxygen, can be renewed by natural processes – *provided* Nature is given the chance. The ecosystem is flexible, but it is balanced, and will continue to function as long as that balance is not upset too drastically. Man is a modifying factor in the equation. Unless he learns to fit into the system more evenly than at present, the equilibrium will be so disturbed that the natural balance will be completely lost. Man must learn to manage his resources – *all* of them – if the present ecosystem, of which Man is part, is to survive.

At the present time, pollution represents a dangerous threat to the stability of the system. If the system is overthrown, another will develop to take its place. However, the new ecosystem could very well be one in which there is no place for Man.

# The
# Spaceship
# Earth

*The four articles in this first section represent part of the range of opinion on the subject of pollution. Our affluent society has certain built-in attitudes, and it is these that emerge as the primary cause for the problem, and the theme for Section 1.*

The Biosphere *is an appropriate introductory article because the reference is international, an immediate reminder of the scope of the problem. Dubos comments on a number of concepts – essential need, environment and conservation. In his opinion essential need is meaningless because it is no longer related to biological requirement, but is a reflection of "social expectation". M. Dubos hits hard at prevalent conservation attitudes. He suggests that conservation activities are*

> *. . . responses to acute crises and usually take the form of disconnected palliative measures designed to minimize social unrest or the depletion of a few natural resources.*

*The author feels that land cannot be returned to its natural state. Man has been involved too long and this would deny the inevitable interrelationship between the environment and man.*

*M. Dubos would like the same kind of utopian visionaries who have built or created great monuments or cities to duplicate this feat in environmental planning.*

*Dr. Paul Ehrlich has written a believable story about the death of the oceans in the summer of 1979. Credibility is achieved by tracing the chain of events that led to the disaster. Emphasis is placed on the cause-effect sequence relating constantly to established socio-economic and political attitudes and traditions. There is, through most of its length, a very matter-of-fact tone. The touches of irony and sarcasm are gloomily amusing. Reality is reimposed in the concluding section where Dr. Ehrlich relates his scenario to the present.*

*The article,* Is a World that Makes Ecological Sense a Dream?, *is based on a vision of Garrett De Bell of the Friends of Earth Society. The dream is rooted in North American rural tradition and is admittedly utopian. As in the Ehrlich scenario, the dream is used to launch an attack on two of the problems caused by pollution – climatic change, and nuclear power generators. Utopia as here developed is quite interesting.*

You and Pollution *focuses attention on the individual as the root cause of pollution in an affluent society. Government and industrial attitudes are only extensions of those of the individual. Man and his institutions are primarily motivated by self, that is, by personal profit. As a result, the effects of technology on society and the environment are neglected.*

*The crisis is heightened by the fact that very few, if any, understand the whole situation. Specialization in both public and private sectors of the society prevents anyone from obtaining more than a fragmented view of aspects outside his own field.*

*A largely ignorant and initially apathetic public has begun to redress the balance, but it is much too soon to know whether the necessary fundamental changes have been made in attitudes.*

# The Biosphere

## René Dubos

All men are migrants from a common origin. Their various races have undergone minor modifications during prehistoric and historic times as a result of the migrations that exposed them to different environmental factors and led them to adopt different ways of life.

But on the whole, their genetic endowment is still much the same as it was several tens of thousands of years ago. Furthermore, there is no indication that it will change significantly in the near future, because the normal process of genetic evolution is much too slow, even though natural selection is still at work. For this reason, human life can be sustained only within the fairly narrow range of physical and chemical limits that fit the anatomic and physiological characteristics of *Homo sapiens*.

The fact that modern man is constantly moving into new environments gives the impression that he is enlarging the range of his biological adaptabilities and thus escaping from the bondage of his evolutionary past. But this is an illusion. Wherever he goes, and whatever he does, man can function only to the extent that he maintains or creates around himself an environment similar to the one within which he evolved.

He moves at the bottom of the sea or in outer space only if he remains linked to the earth by an umbilical cord or is confined within enclosures that almost duplicate the earth's atmosphere. He can survive in polluted environments only if he protects himself by devices that shelter him from these pollutants.

Granted these biological limitations, it remains true on the other hand that man is today as adaptable as he was during the late Stone Age when he established settlements over much of the earth. During the past few decades, countless persons have survived the frightful ordeal of modern warfare or of concentration camps.

Under normal conditions, the biological mechanisms of adaptation are powerfully supplemented by mechanisms that do not require any change in man's biological nature. All over the world, the most crowded, polluted and brutal cities are also the ones that have the greatest appeal and in which population is increasing the fastest. Economic wealth is being produced by men and women working under extreme nervous tension amidst the infernal noise of high-power equipment, typewriters, and telephones, in atmospheres contaminated with chemical fumes or tobacco smoke.

Because man is endowed with such remarkable ability to tolerate conditions profoundly different from the ones under which he evolved, the myth has grown that he can endlessly and safely transform his life and his environment by technological and social innovations; but this is not the case. On the contrary, the very fact that he readily achieves biological and socio-cultural adjustments to many different forms of stress and of undesirable conditions paradoxically spells danger for his individual welfare and for the future of the human race.

Man can achieve some form of tolerance to environmental pollution, crowded and competitive social contacts, the estrangement of life from the natural biological cycles, and other consequences of life in the urban and technological world. This tolerance enables him to overcome effects that are unpleasant or traumatic when first experienced. But in many cases, it is achieved through organic and mental processes which may result in the disorders that so commonly spoil adult life and old age, even in the most prosperous countries.

Man can learn also to tolerate ugly surroundings, dirty skies, and polluted streams. He can live without the fragrance of flowers, the song of birds, the exhilaration of natural scenery and other biological stimuli of the natural world.

This loss of amenities and elimination of the stimuli under which he evolved as a biological and mental being may have no obvious detrimental effect on his physical appearance or his ability to perform as part of the economic or technologic machine. But the ultimate result can be and often is an impoverishment of life, a progressive loss of the qualities that we identify with humanness and a weakening of physical and mental sanity.

Air, water, soil, fire, the rhythms of nature and the variety of living things, are of interest not only as chemical mixtures, physical forces, or biological phenomena; they are the very influences that have shaped human life and thereby created deep human needs that will not change in the foreseeable future. The pathetic week-end exodus to the country or beaches, the fireplaces in overheated city apartments, the sentimental attachment to animal pets or even to plants, testify to the persistence in man of biological and emotional hungers that developed during his evolutionary past and he cannot outgrow.

Like Anteus of the Greek legend, man loses his strength when his feet are off the ground.

---

While the genetic endowment of *Homo sapiens* has not undergone any significant alterations since the late Stone Age, it is obvious that man's interaction with his environment has greatly changed with time and differs from place to place. The reason is that mankind as a whole possesses a wide range of genetic potentialities, most of which remain unexpressed under ordinary conditions. These potentialities are developed through the creative effects of the responses that each person makes to environmental stimuli.

In theory, all human beings have much the same essential biological needs; but in practice actual needs are socially conditioned and therefore differ profoundly from one human group to another. Even food requirements cannot be defined without regard to historical and social factors. The·value of an article of food is not determined only by its content in protein, carbohydrate, fat, vitamins, minerals, and other chemical components.

A particular food has, in addition to its nutritive values, symbolic values which make it either essential or unacceptable to a particular group of persons depending upon their beliefs and past experiences. These symbolic aspects of nutrition are not of importance only among primitive people. Americans are even more reluctant to eat horse meat than Frenchmen are to eat cornbread.

Furthermore, needs are not unchangeable. Some which appear almost essential today may become trivial in another generation, not because man's biological nature will change, but because the social environment usually undergoes rapid and profound modifications. It may turn out for example that the individual motor car will progressively disappear if driving loses its appeal because of traffic congestion or boredom, and if people learn to use more of their leisure time within walking distance of their homes.

The individual detached house so characteristic of the North American continent may also become obsolete once home ownership loses its symbolic meaning of economic and social independence by reason of more generalized prosperity and financial security. Changes in automobile usage and in housing habits would probably have enormous effects on the fate of land areas, as would of course changes in the methods of food production.

The phrase "essential need" is therefore meaningless because in practice people need what they want. As technological civilization develops, needs are determined less and less by the fundamental biological requirements of *Homo sapiens* and more by the social expectations.

These expectations are created by the environment in which man lives and especially in which he has been brought up. The members of a given social group generally come to desire, and consequently develop a need for, whatever is regarded as most desirable by the group. The good life is identified with the satisfaction of these needs whatever their biological utility.

Wants become needs not only for individual persons, but also for whole societies. Elaborate religious institutions and ceremonies were apparently a need for the 13th century European towns, which devoted to the creation of churches and monasteries a percentage of their human and economic resources that appears extravagant to us in relation to the other aspects of medieval life.

Our own societies seem particularly concerned with creating a middle-class materialism. This creates its own pattern of costly demands irrelevant to biological necessity—for example costly carbonated beverages and narcotizing television programmes.

---

The environments men create through their wants constitute to a very large extent the formula of life they transmit to succeeding generations. Thus, in addition to affecting present-day life, the characteristics of the environment condition young people and thereby determine the future of society. It is unfortunate therefore that we know so little and make so little effort to learn how the total environment affects the physical and mental development of children, and how much of the influence persists in adult life.

There is no doubt that the latent potentialities of human beings have a better chance of being realized when the total environment is sufficiently diversified to provide a variety of stimulating experiences, especially for the young. As more persons find the opportunity to express a larger percentage of their biological endowment under diversified conditions, society becomes richer and civilizations continue to unfold.

In contrast, if the surroundings and ways of life are highly stereotyped, the only components of man's nature that can become expressed and flourish are those adapted to the narrow range of prevailing conditions.

Historically, man was very slow to expand his horizons and develop his full genetic potential. Thus, surrounding early man with nature does not seem to guarantee a rich, diverse existence. Furthermore, in some present rural areas of the developed countries, man has produced a monotony of both crops and culture that stifles human development.

The present trends of life in prosperous countries are usually assumed to represent what people want; but in reality the trends are determined by what is available for choice. What people come to want is largely determined by the choices readily available to them early in life. Many children growing up in some of the most prosperous suburbs of industrialized countries may suffer from a critical deprivation of experiences and this determines the triviality of their adult lives. In contrast, some poor areas of the world provide human environments that are so stimulating and diversified that many distinguished adults emerge from them despite the economic poverty of their early years.

There is no doubt, in any case, concerning the sterilizing atmosphere of many modern housing developments which are sanitary and efficient, but hamper the full expression of human potentialities. All over the world, many of these developments are planned as if their only function was to provide disposable cubicles for dispensable people. Irrespective of their genetic constitution, most young people raised in such a featureless environment, and limited to a narrow range of life experiences, will suffer from a kind of deprivation that will cripple them intellectually and mentally.

In judging the human quality of an environment, it is essential to keep in mind that passive exposure to stimuli is not enough to elicit individual development. The stimulus becomes *formative* only if the organism is given a chance to respond to it actively and creatively. Amusement parks and zoological gardens, richly endowed as they may be, are no substitute for situations in which the developing child can gain direct experience of the world through active participation. Juvenile delinquency is probably caused to a very large extent by the failure of the modern world to provide opportunities for the creative expression of physical and mental vigour during a human being's most active period of development.

Man has been highly successful as a biological species because he is extremely adaptable. He can hunt or farm, be a meat-eater or a vegetarian, live in the mountains or by the seashore, be a loner or a team member, function under aristocratic, democratic, or totalitarian institutions, but history shows also that societies that were once efficient, because highly specialized, rapidly collapsed when conditions changed. A highly-specialized society, like a narrow specialist, is rarely adaptable.

Cultural homogenization and social regimentation resulting from the creeping monotony of over-organized and over-technicized life, standardized patterns of education, mass communication and passive entertainment, will make it progressively more difficult to exploit fully the biological richness of the human species and may handicap the further development of civilization.

We must shun uniformity of surroundings as much as absolute conformity in behaviour and tastes. We must strive instead to create as many diversified environments as possible. Richness and diversity of physical and social environments constitute a crucial aspect of functionalism, whether in the planning of rural and urban areas, the design of dwellings, or the management of individual life.

Diversity may result in some loss of mechanical and administrative efficiency and will certainly increase stresses, but the more important goal is to provide the many kinds of soil that will permit the germination of the seeds now dormant in man's nature.

---

It is often assumed that progress depends on man's ability to *conquer* Nature. In reality, there exist throughout mankind biological and emotional needs that require not conquest of Nature, but rather harmonious collaboration with its forces. The ultimate goal of conservation policies should be to manage the environment in such a manner that it contributes to the physical and mental health of man and to the flowering of civilization.

Unfortunately, while there is much know-how concerning certain limited aspects of conservation practices, there is little understanding of what should be conserved and why. In fact, the goal should not be to conserve but rather to guide the orderly evolution of Man–Nature interrelationships.

Conservation certainly implies a balance between the multiple components of nature including man. This is a theory that is difficult to reconcile with the present trends of modern civilization, built on the Faustian concept that man should recognize no limit to his power. Faustian man finds satisfaction in the mastery of the external world and is engaged in endless pursuit of success for success' sake, even when he tries to reach the unattainable. No chance for balance here.

To be compatible with the spirit of modern civilization, the practices of conservation cannot be exclusively or even primarily concerned with saving parts of the natural world or man-made artifacts for the sake of preserving individual specimens of interest or beauty. Their goal should be the maintenance of conditions under which man can develop his most desirable potentialities.

Since man relates to his total environment and especially is shaped by it, conservation implies a quality of relationship rather than a static condition. Man must engage in a creative interplay with his fellows, animals, plants, and all the objects of nature that directly or indirectly affect him, and which he affects.

From the human point of view, the total environment, including the remains of the past, acquires its full significance only when harmoniously integrated with the living tissues of man's life. It can even be demonstrated that because they shape irreversibly all aspects of human development, environmental forces are, so to speak, woven in man's physical and mental fabric.

The ill-defined meaning of the word Nature compounds the difficulty of formulating a scientific basis for the philosophy of conservation. If we mean by nature the environment as it would exist in the absence of man, then very little of it survives. Not even the strictest conservation policies could restore the primeval environment; nor would this be necessarily desirable if it could be done. Nature is never static. Physical forces and living creatures alter it continuously; animals especially modify parts of it to fit their biological and behavioural needs.

---

For animals as well as for men, the kind of environment which is most satisfactory is one with which they are familiar and in which they have introduced modifications that facilitate their biological and social life, such as territorial marks, trails for exploration, access to water supplies, retreats for mating, sheltered areas to protect the young. In general, the ideal conditions imply a complementary relationship between a particular environment and a particular living thing.

Civilized nature should be regarded not as an object to preserve unchanged, not as one to dominate and exploit, but rather as a kind of garden to develop according to its own potentialities and in which human beings develop according to their own genius. Ideally, man and nature should be joined in a non-repressive and creative functioning order.

Nature can be tamed without being destroyed. Unfortunately, the word taming has come to imply subjugating animals and nature. Like men and animals, landscapes tamed in this manner lose their real essence, and become spiritless. To be biologically successful, taming demands the establishment of a relationship that does not deprive the tamed organism – man, animal or nature of the individuality that is the essence of survival.

There are two kinds of satisfactory landscape. One is a landscape as little disturbed as possible by human intervention. The other kind of satisfactory landscape is one created by man and in which he has achieved harmony with natural forces. Most commonly, this has been achieved through centuries of interplay between human societies and the land on which they have settled.

What we long for most often is not nature in the raw, but a landscape adjusted to human limitations and expressing the aspirations of civilized life in its many different forms. For this reason, each people has its preferred landscape, constituting an integration and synthesis of natural forces and of cultural traditions.

Indeed, much of what we regard today as natural environment is in fact a product of history. The valleys of the Nile and Euphrates were shaped by human labour during the Neolithic period. And much of the arable land all over the world is also the product of man's management of the primeval forest.

Many of the plants now considered typical of the Mediterranean landscape, the olive tree for example, were in fact introduced from Iran. The tulip, which is now such a characteristic of the Netherlands, was first brought there from Turkey as late as the 16th century.

Irrespective of social changes, cities and their streets, the highways linking them, as well as the countryside surrounding them, also retain traces of the character imposed on them by early historical influences. The future development of new cities, especially in the U.S.A., is bound to be constrained by the grid-iron pattern and the network of highways that shaped their early growth.

Since most of the environment as it exists today is a creation of man, and in turn influences the subsequent development of human societies, environmental quality must take into consideration not so much the preservation of the natural state, as the effects of the environment on the future of civilized life.

From this point of view, the situation looks very dark in most parts of the world. Everywhere, societies seem willing to accept ugliness for the sake of increase in economic wealth. Whether natural or humanized, the landscape retains its beauty only in the areas that are not valuable for industrial and economic exploitation.

The change from wilderness to dump heap symbolizes at present the course of technological civilization. Yet the material wealth we are creating will not be worth having if creation entails the raping of nature and the destruction of environmental charm.

In the past, the primeval wilderness progressively evolved into a humanized form of nature through the continuous "wooing" of the earth by peasants, monks, and princes. We must now learn to convert the drab wilderness generated by technology into a new kind of urbanized and industrialized nature worthy of being called civilized.

In the huge urban areas of the modern world we must supply the inhabitants with something more than amusement parks, highways for sightseers and paved grounds for weekend campers. No social philosophy of urbanization can be successful it if does not deal with urban man as part of the highly integrated web which unites all forms of life.

There have been many large cities in the past, but until recent times their inhabitants were able to maintain fairly close and direct contacts with the countryside or with the sea, and thus could satisfy the physiological and psychological needs acquired during the human past. Historical experience, especially during the 19th century, shows that urban populations are apt to develop ugly tempers when completely deprived of such contacts. Saving nature in both its wild and humanized aspects is thus an essential part of urban planning.

Wherever man has been successful in "wooing" the land and keeping it biologically workable, success has resulted from his ability and willingness to plan his creations within the constraints determined by climate, topography, and other local characteristics of Nature. In the past, this was also true of cities which were planned in accord with certain geographical imperatives.

Modern cities are in contrast developing without any regard to physical and biological constraints and only under the influence of economic and political imperatives. The belief that man can "master" the environment and achieve independence of his innate biological limitations has generated the impression that there is no need for disciplines in the development of cities. Most urban problems derive precisely from such a misapplied interpretation of freedom.

Town planning as well as country planning will not be successful until we learn again to recognize and accept the restraints that are inherent in man's biological nature and in geographical conditions. In fact the whole concept of planning the use of our environment, or perhaps what is better described in French as "aménagement du territoire," is only emerging as a new discipline and it is high time that it be developed all over the world on sound ecological principles.

Rational environmental planning cannot be done by acting under the pressure of emergency as is now the general practice. Unfortunately, the construction of great dams all over the world is prompted not by comprehensive, integrated programmes of water and land use but by the threat of floods or of water shortages. Policies for the control of soil erosion are enacted only after irreversible damage has been done.

There is a general awareness of the dangers posed by noise, environmental pollution, and the misuse of drugs, but effective measures are rarely taken before some catastrophe creates an atmosphere of panic. In fact, most environmental programmes emerge as responses to acute crises and usually take the form of disconnected palliative measures designed to minimize social unrest or the depletion of a few natural resources.

For lack of adequate knowledge, the environment is being manipulated almost exclusively on the basis of technological criteria without much concern for its biological and psychological effects. These effects should be considered not only in the here and now, but in their long-range consequences and in their relevance to mankind as a whole.

Before long, all parts of the globe will have been occupied or exploited by man and the supply of many natural resources will have become critical. Careful husbandry of the spaceship Earth rather than exploitation of natural resources, will then be the key to human survival.

Developing stations in outer space or on the bottom of oceans will not modify significantly if at all the physical limits of human existence. Man emerged on the earth, evolved under its influence, was shaped by it, and biologically he is bound to it forever. He may dream of stars and engage in casual flirtations with other worlds, but he will remain wedded to the earth, his sole source of sustenance.

As the world population increases, the topographical limitations of the spaceship Earth and the inevitable exhaustion of its natural resources will inevitably require that its economy be based on strict ecological principles. This imperative necessity, however, is not yet widely recognized. The very word ecology (the interrelationships of organisms and their environments) was introduced into the scientific language only 100 years ago by Ernst Haeckel, the German biologist, so recent is the awareness that all components of nature are interwoven in a single pattern and that we too are part of the pattern!

Until now, man has behaved as if the areas available to him were unlimited, and as if these were infinite reservoirs of air, soil, water, and other resources. He could do this with relative impunity in the past because there was always some other place where he could go, start a new life, and engage in any kind of adventure that he chose.

Since the evolutionary and historical experiences of man are woven in his mental fabric he naturally finds it difficult *not* to behave as a nomad and hunter. It is not natural for him to rest quietly in a corner of the earth and husband it carefully. His thoughtlessness in provoking ecological situations that are potentially dangerous originates partly from the fact that he has not yet learned to live within the constraints of his spaceship.

The ecological attitude is so unfamiliar, even to many scientists, that it is often taken to imply acceptance of a completely static system. Students of human sociology have expressed concern lest the ecologist's professional interest in the well-balanced, smoothly-functioning, steady-state ecosystem of the pond be extended to the whole earth and its human population. They are right in emphasizing that man's relation to his total environment cannot be regarded as a steady-state ecosystem because this would imply that the human adventure has come to an end.

The physical forces of the environment are forever changing, slowly but inexorably. Furthermore, all forms of life including human life are continuously evolving and thereby making their own contribution to environmental changes. Finally it seems to be one of man's fundamental needs to search endlessly for new environments and for new adventures. There is no possibility therefore of maintaining a *status quo*.

Even if we had enough learning and wisdom to achieve at any given time a harmonious state of ecological equilibrium between mankind and the other components of the spaceship Earth, it would be a dynamic equilibrium, and this would be compatible with man's continuing development.

The important question is whether the interplay between man and his natural and social surroundings will be controlled by blind forces as seems to be the case for most if not all animal species, or whether it can be guided by deliberate, rational judgements.

Admittedly, all of man's biological evolution so far and much of his history have been the result of accidents or blind choices. Many deliberate actions have had consequences that had not been foreseen and often proved to be unfortunate. In fact, most of the environmental problems which now plague technological civilization derive from discoveries and decisions made to solve other problems and to enlarge human life.

The internal combustion engine, synthetic detergents, durable pesticides and medicinal drugs, were introduced with a useful purpose in mind, but some of their side effects have been calamitous. Efficient methods of printing have made good books available at low prices, but are cluttering mail boxes with despicable publications and useless advertisements; these burden wastebaskets with mountains of refuse which must be burned and thus pollute the air.

Waste disposal is becoming as critical as resource production. It is obvious, from the law of the conservation of matter, that waste is produced exactly in the amount that resources are used. What is not so obvious is that, in the long run, the reverse must also be true: resource production depends upon the utilization of waste. Otherwise man will convert the biosphere into a global dump.

Waste that nature cannot process accumulates and pollutes the environment. Converting such waste into a usable form not only solves a problem of pollution, but also contributes positively to environmental quality and the production of future resources.

Like animal life, human life is affected by evolutionary forces that blindly fit the organism to its environments. Human history, however, involves also the unfolding of visionary imaginings. Creating a desirable future demands more than foresight; it requires vision.

The 18th century philosophers of the Enlightenment had imagined new ways of life long before there was any factual basis for their vision. They prepared the blueprint for most of what is new and desirable in modern societies on the faith that objective knowledge, scientific technology, and social reforms, could some day liberate human beings from fear and destitution. Throughout human history, progress has been a movement toward imagined utopian goals; the realization of these aims has in turn inspired new goals.

Mankind's greatest achievements are the products of vision. One need think only of the marvellous parks, gardens, and monuments that have survived from all great civilizations to realize the creative force of a long-range view in shaping desirable humanized environments.

The great parks and gardens all over the world originated from that extraordinary sense which is peculiar to man, the imaginary vision of things to come. For example, several books by European landscape architects of the 18th century show drawings of parks as they appeared at the time of their creation, with the naked banks of newly-created brooks and lakes, among puny trees and shrubs.

In these drawings, the landscapes have an abstract and cold elegance, but lack substance or atmosphere. One has to assume that the landscape architects had composed the expanses of water, lawns, and flowers to fit the silhouettes of trees and the masses of shrubbery not as these components of the landscape existed when first organized but as they were to become with the passage of time.

The architects had visualized the future appearance of their intellectual imaginings and planned their actual designs and plantings so as to give scope to the creative effects of natural forces. Similar visionary anticipations account for most of the great urban sites and vistas throughout the world.

While the great gardens, parks, and urban vistas created by past civilizations still delight our senses and minds, other kinds of landscapes must be conceived to meet present and future needs. The old country roads, lined with stately trees, provided poetic and practical shelter for the man on foot or horseback and for slow-moving coaches.

A modern highway, however, must be designed in such a manner that horizons, curves, trees and other objects of view are related to the physiological needs and limitations of motorists moving at high speed. The evolution from parkways and super highways involves aesthetic factors based on physiological imperatives, as much as economic and technologic considerations.

Envisioning an environment satisfying the needs of an immense technological society is of course vastly more complicated than visualizing the future appearance of a park or designing a super highway. But certain principles hold true for all environmental planning, because they are based on the unchangeable and universal aspects of man's nature.

---

On the one hand, the genetic endowment of *Homo sapiens* has changed only in minor details since the Stone Age, and there is no chance that it can be significantly, usefully, or safely modified in the foreseeable future. This genetic permanency defines the human race, and determines the physiological limits beyond which human life cannot be safely altered by social and technological innovations. In the final analysis, the frontiers of cultural and technological development are determined by man's own biological frontiers and therefore by the genetic constitution he acquired during the evolutionary past.

On the other hand, mankind has a large reserve of potentialities that become expressed only to the extent that circumstances are favourable. The physical surroundings condition not only the biological aspects of phenotypic expressions but also their mental aspects. Environmental planning can thus play a key role in enabling human beings to realize their potentialities. One can take it for granted that there is a better chance to convert these potentialities into actual realizations when the physical environment is sufficiently diversified to provide a variety of stimulating experiences and opportunities, especially for the young.

Any change in mental attitude and in ways of life becomes incorporated in the human group concerned through socio-cultural mechanisms, and from then on it conditions the future development of the group. Socio-cultural evolution is as much under the influence of the environment as is biological evolution, and almost as irreversible.

Planning for the future demands an ecological attitude based on the assumption that man will continuously bring about evolutionary changes through his creative potentialities. The constant interaction between man and environment inevitably implies continuous alterations of both – alterations that should always remain within the constraints imposed by the laws of Nature and by the unchangeable biological and mental characteristics of man's nature.

# Eco-catastrophe

## Paul Ehrlich

I

The end of the ocean came late in the summer of 1979, and it came even more rapidly than the biologists had expected. There had been signs for more than a decade, commencing with the discovery in 1968 that DDT slows down photosynthesis in marine plant life. It was announced in a short paper in the technical journal, Science, but to ecologists it smacked of doomsday. They knew that all life in the sea depends on photosynthesis, the chemical process by which green plants bind the sun's energy and make it available to living things. And they knew that DDT and similar chlorinated hydrocarbons had polluted the entire surface of the earth, including the sea.

But that was only the first of many signs. There had been the final gasp of the whaling industry in 1973, and the end of the Peruvian anchovy fishery in 1975. Indeed, a score of other fisheries had disappeared quietly from over-exploitation and various eco-catastrophes by 1977. The term "eco-catastrophe" was coined by a California ecologist in 1969 to describe the most spectacular of man's attacks on the systems which sustain his life. He drew his inspiration from the Santa Barbara offshore oil disaster of that year, and from the news which spread among naturalists that virtually all of the Golden State's seashore bird life was doomed because of chlorinated hydrocarbon interference with its reproduction. Eco-catastrophes in the sea became increasingly common in the early 1970's. Mysterious "blooms" of previously rare micro-organisms began to appear in offshore waters. Red tides – killer outbreaks of a minute single-celled plant – returned to the Florida Gulf coast and were sometimes accompanied by tides of other exotic hues.

It was clear by 1975 that the entire ecology of the ocean was changing. A few types of phytoplankton were becoming resistant to chlorinated hydrocarbons and were gaining the upper hand. Changes in the phytoplankton community led inevitably to changes in the community of zooplankton, the tiny animals which eat the phytoplankton. These changes were passed on up the chains of life in the ocean to the herring, plaice, cod and tuna. As the diversity of life in the ocean diminished, its stability also decreased.

Other changes had taken place by 1975. Most ocean fishes that returned to fresh water to breed, like the salmon, had become extinct, their breeding streams so dammed up and polluted that their powerful homing instinct only resulted in suicide. Many fishes and shellfishes that bred in restricted areas along the coasts followed them as onshore pollution escalated.

By 1977 the annual yield of fish from the sea was down to 30 million metric tons, less than one-half the per capita catch of a decade earlier. This helped malnutrition to escalate sharply in a world where an estimated 50 million people per year were already dying of starvation. The United Nations attempted to get all chlorinated hydrocarbon insecticides banned on a worldwide basis, but the move was defeated by the United States. This opposition was generated primarily by the American petrochemical industry, operating hand in glove with its subsidiary, the United States Department of Agriculture. Together they persuaded the government to oppose the U.N. move – which was not difficult since most Americans believed that Russia and China were more in need of fish products than was the United States. The United Nations also attempted to get fishing nations to adopt strict and enforced catch limits to preserve dwindling stocks. This move was blocked by Russia, who, with the most modern electronic equipment, was in the best position to glean what was left in the sea. It was, curiously, on the very day in 1977 when the Soviet Union announced its refusal that another ominous article appeared in Science. It announced that incident solar radiation had been so reduced by worldwide air pollution that serious effects on the world's vegetation could be expected.

## II

Apparently it was a combination of ecosystem destabilization, sunlight reduction, and a rapid escalation in chlorinated hydrocarbon pollution from massive Thanodrin applications which triggered the ultimate catastrophe. Seventeen huge Soviet-financed Thanodrin plants were operating in underdeveloped countries by 1978. They had been part of a massive Russian "aid offensive" designed to fill the gap caused by the collapse of America's ballyhooed "Green Revolution."

It became apparent in the early '70s that the "Green Revolution" was more talk than substance. Distribution of high yield "miracle" grain seeds had caused temporary local spurts in agricultural production.

Simultaneously, excellent weather had produced record harvests. The combination permitted bureaucrats, especially in the United States Department of Agriculture and the Agency for International Development (AID), to reverse their previous pessimism and indulge in an outburst of optimistic propaganda about staving off famine. They raved about the approaching transformation of agriculture in the underdeveloped countries (UDCs). The reason for the propaganda reversal was never made clear. Most historians agree that a combination of utter ignorance of ecology, a desire to justify past errors, and pressure from agro-industry (which was eager to sell pesticides, fertilizers, and farm machinery to the UDCs and agencies helping the UDCs) was behind the campaign. Whatever the motivation, the results were clear. Many concerned people, lacking the expertise to see through the Green Revolution drivel, relaxed. The population-food crisis was "solved".

But reality was not long in showing itself. Local famine persisted in northern India even after good weather brought an end to the ghastly Bihar famine of the mid-'60s. East Pakistan was next, followed by a resurgence of general famine in northern India. Other foci of famine rapidly developed in Indonesia, the Philippines, Malawi, the Congo, Egypt, Colombia, Ecuador, Honduras, the Dominican Republic, and Mexico.

Everywhere hard realities destroyed the illusion of the Green Revolution. Yields dropped as the progressive farmers who had first accepted the new seeds found that their higher yields brought lower prices – effective demand (hunger plus cash) was not sufficient in poor countries to keep prices up. Less progressive farmers, observing this, refused to make the extra effort required to cultivate the "miracle" grains. Transport systems proved inadequate to bring the necessary fertilizer to the fields where the new and extremely fertilizer-sensitive grains were being grown. The same systems were also inadequate to move produce to markets. Fertilizer plants were not built fast enough, and most of the underdeveloped countries could not scrape together funds to purchase supplies, even on concessional terms. Finally, the inevitable happened, and pests began to reduce yields in even the most carefully cultivated fields. Among the first were the famous "miracle rats" which invaded Philippine "miracle rice" fields early in 1969. They were quickly followed by many insects and viruses, thriving on the relatively pest-susceptible new grains, encouraged by the vast and dense plantings, and rapidly acquiring resistance to the chemicals used against them. As chaos spread until even the most obtuse agriculturists and economists realized that the Green Revolution had turned brown, the Russians stepped in.

In retrospect it seems incredible that the Russians, with the American mistakes known to them, could launch an even more incompetent program of aid to the underdeveloped world. Indeed, in the early 1970's there were cynics in the United States who claimed that outdoing the stupidity of American foreign aid would be physically impossible. Those critics were, however, obviously unaware that the Russians had been busily destroying their own environment for many years. The virtual disappearance of sturgeon from Russian rivers caused a great shortage of caviar by 1970. A standard joke among Russian scientists at that time was that they had created an artificial caviar which was indistinguishable from the real thing – except by taste. At any rate the Soviet Union, observing with interest the progressive deterioration of relations between the UDCs and the United States, came up with a solution. It had recently developed what it claimed was the ideal insecticide, a highly lethal chlorinated hydrocarbon complexed with a special agent for penetrating the external skeletal armor of insects. Announcing that the new pesticide, called Thanodrin, would truly produce a Green Revolution, the Soviets entered into negotiations with various UDCs for the construction of massive Thanodrin factories. The USSR would bear all the costs; all it wanted in return were certain trade and military concessions.

It is interesting now, with the perspective of years, to examine in some detail the reasons why the UDCs welcomed the Thanodrin plan with such open arms. Government officials in these countries ignored the protests of their own scientists that Thanodrin would not solve the problems which plagued them. The governments now knew that the basic cause of their problems was overpopulation, and that these problems had been exacerbated by the dullness, daydreaming, and cupidity endemic to all governments. They knew that only population control and limited development aimed primarily at agriculture could have spared them the horrors they now faced. They knew it, but they were not about to admit it. How much easier it was simply to accuse the Americans of failing to give them proper aid; how much simpler to accept the Russian panacea.

And then there was the general worsening of relations between the United States and the UDCs. Many things had contributed to this. The situation in America in the first half of the 1970's deserves our close scrutiny. Being more dependent on imports for raw materials than the Soviet Union, the United States had, in the early 1970's, adopted more and more heavy-handed policies in order to insure continuing supplies. Military adventures in Asia and Latin America had further lessened the international credibility of the United States as a great defender of freedom – an image which had begun to deteriorate rapidly during the pointless and fruitless Viet-Nam conflict. At home, acceptance of the carefully manufactured image lessened dramatically, as even the more romantic and chauvinistic citizens began to understand the role of the military and the industrial system in what John Kenneth Galbraith had aptly named "The New Industrial State".

At home in the USA the early '70s were traumatic times. Racial violence grew and the habitability of the cities diminished, as nothing substantial was done to ameliorate either racial inequities or urban blight. Welfare rolls grew as automation and general technological progress forced more and more people into the category of "unemployable". Simultaneously a taxpayers' revolt occurred. Although there was not enough money to build the schools, roads, water systems, sewage systems, jails, hospitals, urban transit lines, and all the other amenities needed to support a burgeoning population, Americans refused to tax themselves more heavily. Starting in Youngstown, Ohio in 1969 and followed closely by Richmond, California, community after community was forced to close its schools or curtail educational operations for lack of funds. Water supplies, already marginal in quality and quantity in many places by 1970, deteriorated quickly. Water rationing occurred in 1723 municipalities in the summer of 1974, and hepatitis and epidemic dysentery rates climbed about 500 per cent between 1970-1974.

### III

Air pollution continued to be the most obvious manifestation of environmental deterioration. It was, by 1972, quite literally in the eyes of all Americans. The year 1973 saw not only the New York and Los Angeles smog disasters, but also the publication of the Surgeon General's massive report on air pollution and health. The public had been partially prepared for the worst by the publicity given to the U.N. pollution conference held in 1972. Deaths in the late '60s caused by smog were well known to scientists, but the public had ignored them because they mostly involved the early demise of the old and sick rather than people dropping dead on the freeways. But suddenly our citizens were faced with nearly 200,000 corpses and massive documentation that they could be the next to die from respiratory disease. They were not ready for that scale of disaster. After all, the U.N. conference had not predicted that accumulated air pollution would make the planet uninhabitable until almost 1990. The population was terrorized as TV screens became filled with scenes of horror from the disaster areas. Especially vivid was NBC's coverage of hundreds of unattended people choking out their lives outside of New York's hospitals. Terms like nitrogen oxide, acute bronchitis and cardiac arrest began to have real meaning for most Americans.

The ultimate horror was the announcement that chlorinated hydrocarbons were now a major constituent of air pollution in all American cities. Autopsies of smog disaster victims revealed an average chlorinated hydrocarbon load in fatty tissue equivalent to 26 parts per million of DDT. In October, 1973, the Department of Health, Education and Welfare announced studies which showed unequivocally that increasing death rates from hypertension, cirrhosis of the liver, liver cancer and a series of other diseases had resulted from the chlorinated hydrocarbon load. They estimated that Americans born since 1946 (when DDT usage began) now had a life expectancy of only 49 years, and predicted that if current patterns continued, this expectancy would reach 42 years by 1980, when it might level out. Plunging insurance stocks triggered a stock market panic. The president of Velsicol, Inc., a major pesticide producer, went on television to "publicly eat a teaspoonful of DDT" (it was really powdered milk) and announce that HEW had been infiltrated by Communists. Other giants of the petrochemical industry, attempting to dispute the indisputable evidence, launched a massive pressure campaign on Congress to force HEW to "get out of agriculture's business." They were aided by the agro-chemical journals, which had decades of experience in misleading the public about the benefits and dangers of pesticides. But by now the public realized that it had been duped. The Nobel Prize for medicine and physiology was given to Drs. J. L. Radomski and W. B. Deichmann, who in the late 1960's had pioneered in the documentation of the long-term lethal effects of chlorinated hydrocarbons. A Presidential Commission with unimpeachable credentials directly accused the agro-chemical complex of "condemning many millions of Americans to an early death." The year 1973 was the year in which Americans finally came to understand the direct threat to their existence posed by environmental deterioration.

And 1973 was also the year in which most people finally comprehended the indirect threat. Even the president of Union Oil Company and several other industrialists publicly stated their concern over the reduction of bird populations which had resulted from pollution by DDT and other chlorinated hydrocarbons. Insect populations boomed because they were resistant to most pesticides and had been freed, by the incompetent use of those pesticides, from most of their natural enemies. Rodents swarmed over crops, multiplying rapidly in the absence of predatory birds. The effect of pests on the wheat crop was especially disastrous in the summer of 1973, since that was also the year of the great drought. Most of us can remember the shock which greeted the announcement by atmospheric physicists that the shift of the jet stream which had caused the drought was probably permanent. It signalled the birth of the Midwestern desert. Man's air-polluting activities had by then caused gross changes in climatic patterns. The news, of course, played hell with commodity and stock markets. Food prices skyrocketed, as savings were poured into hoarded canned goods. Official assurances that food supplies would remain ample fell on deaf ears, and even the government showed signs of nervousness when California migrant field workers went out on strike again in protest against the continued use of pesticides by growers. The strike burgeoned into farm burning and riots. The workers, calling themselves "The Walking Dead," demanded immediate compensation for their shortened lives, and crash research programs to attempt to lengthen them.

It was in the same speech in which President Edward Kennedy, after much delay, finally declared a national emergency and called out the National Guard to harvest California's crops, that the first mention of population control was made. Kennedy pointed out that the United States would no longer be able to offer any food aid to other nations and was likely to suffer food shortages herself. He suggested that, in view of the manifest failure of the Green Revolution, the only hope of the UDCs lay in population control. His statement, you will recall, created an uproar in the underdeveloped countries. Newspaper editorials accused the United States of wishing to prevent small countries from becoming large nations and thus threatening American hegemony. Politicians asserted that President Kennedy was a "creature of the giant drug combine" that wished to shove its pills down every woman's throat.

Among Americans, religious opposition to population control was very slight. Industry in general also backed the idea. Increasing poverty in the UDCs was both destroying markets and threatening supplies of raw materials. The seriousness of the raw material situation had been brought home during the Congressional Hard Resources hearings in 1971. The exposure of the ignorance of the cornucopian economists had been quite a spectacle – a spectacle brought into virtually every American's home in living color. Few would forget the distinguished geologist from the University of California who suggested that economists be legally required to learn at least the most elementary facts of geology. Fewer still would forget that an equally distinguished Harvard economist added that they might be required to learn some economics, too. The overall message was clear: America's resource situation was bad and bound to get worse. The hearings had led to a bill requiring the Departments of State, Interior, and Commerce to set up a joint resource procurement council with the express purpose of "insuring that proper consideration of American resource needs be an integral part of American foreign policy."

## IV

Suddenly the United States discovered that it had a national consensus: population control was the only possible salvation of the underdeveloped world. But that same consensus led to heated debate. How could the UDCs be persuaded to limit their populations, and should not the United States lead the way by limiting its own? Members of the intellectual community wanted America to set an example. They pointed out that the United States was in the midst of a new baby boom: her birth rate, well over 20 per thousand per year, and her growth rate of over one per cent per annum were among the very highest of the developed countries. They detailed the deterioration of the American physical and psychic environments, the growing health threats, the impending food shortages, and the insufficiency of funds for desperately needed public works. They contended that the nation was clearly unable or unwilling to properly care for the people it already had. What possible reason could there be, they queried, for adding any more? Besides, who would listen to requests by the United States for population control when that nation did not control her own profligate reproduction?

Those who opposed population controls for the U.S. were equally vociferous. The military-industrial complex, with its all-too-human mixture of ignorance and avarice, still saw strength and prosperity in numbers. Baby food magnates, already worried by the growing nitrate pollution of their products, saw their market disappearing. Steel manufacturers saw a decrease in aggregate demand and slippage for that holy of holies, the Gross National Product. And military men saw, in the growing population-food-environment crisis, a serious threat to their carefully nurtured Cold War. In the end, of course, economic arguments held sway, and the "inalienable right of every American couple to determine the size of its family," a freedom invented for the occasion in the early '70s, was not compromised.

The population control bill, which was passed by Congress early in 1974, was quite a document, nevertheless. On the domestic front, it authorized an increase from 100 to 150 million dollars in funds for "family planning" activities. This was made possible by a general feeling in the country that the growing army on welfare needed family planning. But the gist of the bill was a series of measures designed to impress the need for population control on the UDCs. All American aid to countries with overpopulation problems was required by law to consist in part of population control assistance. In order to receive any assistance each nation was required not only to accept the population control aid, but also to match it according to a complex formula. "Overpopulation" itself was defined by a formula based on U.N. statistics, and the UDCs were required not only to accept aid, but also to show progress in reducing birth rates. Every five years the status of the aid program for each nation was to be re-evaluated.

The reaction to the announcement of this program dwarfed the response to President Kennedy's speech. A coalition of UDCs attempted to get the U.N. General Assembly to condemn the United States as a "genetic aggressor." Most damaging of all to the American cause was the famous "25 Indians and a dog" speech by Mr. Shankarnarayan, Indian Ambassador to the U.N. Shankarnarayan pointed out that for several decades the United States, with less than six per cent of the people of the world, had consumed roughly 50 per cent of the raw materials used every year. He described vividly America's contribution to worldwide environmental deterioration, and he scathingly denounced the miserly record of United States foreign aid as "unworthy of a fourth-rate power, let alone the most powerful nation on earth."

It was the climax of his speech, however, which most historians claim once and for all destroyed the image of the United States. Shankarnarayan informed the assembly that the average American family dog was fed more animal protein per week than the average Indian got in a month. "How do you justify taking fish from protein-starved Peruvians and feeding them to your animals?" he asked. "I contend," he concluded, "that the birth of an American baby is a greater disaster for the world than that of 25 Indian babies." When the applause had died away, Mr. Sorensen, the American representative, made a speech which said essentially that "other countries look after their own self-interest, too." When the vote came, the United States was condemned.

V

This condemnation set the tone of U.S.-UDC relations at the time the Russian Thanodrin proposal was made. The proposal seemed to offer the masses in the UDCs an opportunity to save themselves and humiliate the United States at the same time; and in human affairs, as we all know, biological realities could never interfere with such an opportunity. The scientists were silenced, the politicians said yes, the Thanodrin plants were built, and the results were what any beginning ecology student could have predicted. At first Thanodrin seemed to offer excellent control of many pests. True, there was a rash of human fatalities from improper use of the lethal chemical, but, as Russian technical advisors were prone to note, these were more than compensated for by increased yields. Thanodrin use skyrocketed throughout the underdeveloped world. The Mikoyan design group developed a dependable, cheap agricultural aircraft which the Soviets donated to the effort in large numbers. MIG sprayers became even more common in UDCs than MIG interceptors.

Then the troubles began. Insect strains with cuticles resistant to Thanodrin penetration began to appear. And as streams, rivers, fish culture ponds and onshore waters became rich in Thanodrin, more fisheries began to disappear. Bird populations were decimated. The sequence of events was standard for broadcast use of a synthetic pesticide: great success at first, followed by removal of natural enemies and development of resistance by the pest. Populations of crop-eating insects in areas treated with Thanodrin made steady comebacks and soon became more abundant than ever. Yields plunged, while farmers in their desperation increased the Thanodrin dose and shortened the time between treatments. Death from Thanodrin poisoning became common. The first violent incident occurred in the Canete Valley of Peru, where farmers had suffered a similar chlorinated hydrocarbon disaster in the mid-'50s. A Russian advisor serving as an agricultural pilot was assaulted and killed by a mob of enraged farmers in January, 1978. Trouble spread rapidly during 1978, especially after the word got out that two years earlier Russia herself had banned the use of Thanodrin at home because of its serious effects on ecological systems. Suddenly Russia, and not the United States, was the *bête noir* in the UDCs. "Thanodrin parties" became epidemic, with farmers, in their ignorance, dumping carloads of Thanodrin concentrate into the sea. Russian advisors fled, and four of the Thanodrin plants were leveled to the ground. Destruction of the plants in Rio and Calcutta led to hundreds of thousands of gallons of Thanodrin concentrate being dumped directly into the sea.

Mr. Shankarnarayan again rose to address the U.N., but this time it was Mr. Potemkin, representative of the Soviet Union, who was on the hot seat. Mr. Potemkin heard his nation described as the greatest mass killer of all time as Shankarnarayan predicted at least 30 million deaths from crop failures due to overdependence on Thanodrin. Russia was accused of "chemical aggression," and the General Assembly, after a weak reply by Potemkin, passed a vote of censure.

It was in January, 1979, that huge blooms of a previously unknown variety of diatom were reported off the coast of Peru. The blooms were accompanied by a massive die-off of sea life and of the pathetic remainder of the birds which had once feasted on the anchovies of the area. Almost immediately another huge bloom was reported in the Indian ocean, centering around the Seychelles, and then a third in the South Atlantic off the African coast. Both of these were accompanied by spectacular die-offs of marine animals. Even more ominous were growing reports of fish and bird kills at oceanic points where there were no spectacular blooms. Biologists were soon able to explain the phenomena: the diatom had evolved an enzyme which broke down Thanodrin; that enzyme also produced a breakdown product which interfered with the transmission of nerve impulses, and was therefore lethal to animals. Unfortunately, the biologists could suggest no way of repressing the poisonous diatom bloom in time. By September, 1979, all important animal life in the sea was extinct. Large areas of coastline had to be evacuated, as windrows of dead fish created a monumental stench.

But stench was the least of man's problems. Japan and China were faced with almost instant starvation from a total loss of the seafood on which they were so dependent. Both blamed Russia for their situation and demanded immediate mass shipments of food. Russia had none to send. On October 13, Chinese armies attacked Russia on a broad front. . . .

## VI

A pretty grim scenario. Unfortunately, we're a long way into it already. Everything mentioned as happening before 1970 has actually occurred; much of the rest is based on projections of trends already appearing.

Evidence that pesticides have long-term lethal effects on human beings has started to accumulate, and recently Robert Finch, Secretary of the Department of Health, Education and Welfare expressed his extreme apprehension about the pesticide situation. Simultaneously the petro-chemical industry continues its unconscionable poison-peddling. For instance, Shell Chemical has been carrying on a high-pressure campaign to sell the insecticide Azodrin to farmers as a killer of cotton pests. They continue their program even though they know that Azodrin is not only ineffective, but often *increases* the pest density. They've covered them-selves nicely in an advertisement which states, "Even if an overpowering migration [sic] develops, the flexibility of Azodrin lets you regain con-trol fast. Just increase the dosage according to label recommendations." It's a great game – get people to apply the poison and kill the natural enemies of the pests. Then blame the increased pests on "migration" and sell even more pesticide!

Right now fisheries are being wiped out by over-exploitation, made easy by modern electronic equipment. The companies producing the equipment know this. They even boast in advertising that only their equipment will keep fishermen in business until the final kill. Profits must obviously be maximized in the short run. Indeed, Western society is in the process of completing the rape and murder of the planet for economic gain. And, sadly, most of the rest of the world is eager for the opportunity to emulate our behavior. But the underdeveloped peoples will be denied that opportunity – the days of plunder are drawing inexorably to a close.

Most of the people who are going to die in the greatest cataclysm in the history of man have already been born. More than three and a half billion people already populate our moribund globe, and about half of them are hungry. Some 10 to 20 million will starve to death *this year*. In spite of this, the population of the earth will increase by 70 million souls in 1969. For mankind has artificially lowered the death rate of the human population, while in general birth rates have remained high. With the input side of the population system in high gear and the output side slowed down, our fragile planet has filled with people at an in-credible rate. It took several million years for the population to reach a total of two billion people in 1930, while a *second two billion will have been added by 1975!* By that time some experts feel that food shortages will have escalated the present level of world hunger and starvation into famines of unbelievable proportions. Other experts, more optimistic, think the ultimate food-population collision will not occur until the decade of the 1980's. Of course more massive famine may be avoided if other events cause a prior rise in the human death rate.

Both worldwide plague and thermonuclear war are made more probable as population growth continues. These, along with famine, make up the trio of potential "death rate solutions" to the population problem—solutions in which the birth rate–death rate imbalance is redressed by a rise in the death rate rather than by a lowering of the birth rate. Make no mistake about it, *the imbalance will be redressed.* The shape of the population growth curve is one familiar to the biologist. It is the outbreak part of an outbreak-crash sequence. A population grows rapidly in the presence of abundant resources, finally runs out of food or some other necessity, and crashes to a low level or extinction. Man is not only running out of food, he is also destroying the life support systems of the Spaceship Earth. The situation was recently summarized very succinctly: "It is the top of the ninth inning. Man, always a threat at the plate, has been hitting Nature hard. It is important to remember, however, that NATURE BATS LAST."

# Is a World That Makes Ecological Sense Only a Dream?

Imagine a world that makes ecological sense.

Imagine the world has at last come to realize that earth is only, after all, a spaceship, and that mankind's continued survival in the infinite void of the universe depends on his maintenance of the life-support systems on that ship.

Overpopulation has been recognized for the mindless catastrophe that it is, and world population figures are steadily edging back from the present 3.5 billion to something less than 1 billion, a population that can be supported at a standard of living roughly equivalent to that enjoyed in Northern Europe.

Western society has at last come to realize what the East has understood all along – that there is a distinction to be made between "standard of living," and "quality of life," and we have opted to pursue the latter.

This has meant that production and consumption are no longer the sacrosanct indicators of the health of our economy. Instead, in our spaceship economy, what we are primarily concerned with is stock maintenance, and any technological development which results in less consumption is clearly a gain.

We have recognized that growth for growth's sake is the rationale of the cancer cell.

Garrett De Bell of the Friends of Earth Society had such a dream not long ago, and this is what he saw:

"You can imagine hearing someone saying, 'Remember the subdivision that used to be where that orange grove is?' You can see a web of parks throughout the cities replacing the freeways and streets that once dominated.

"You can see agriculture becoming diversified again, with a great variety of crops being grown together, replacing the old reliance on mass-produced single crop operations that are highly dependent on pesticides, machines and cheap farm labor.

"The traditional values of North American rural life come back and many people grow their own food on rural holdings and with a better quality of existence for the farm workers – and for everyone else."

De Bell saw an end to the kinds of contradictions in our way of living that have us burning fossil fuels and exploiting atomic energy – while at the same time polluting the air and water with organic and radioactive wastes – to provide electricity to run escalators and other labor-saving devices. Labor-saving devices that make us fat and weak and send us to the electric exercising machines and to the supermarket for calorie-free soft drinks.

We find that with reduced consumption of electricity, there is less need to build dams on wild rivers, to pollute the air with the waste from oxidized fossil fuels and poison the ecosphere with atomic wastes.

With the end to conspicuous consumption we have more leisure time, a shorter work week. There are fewer automobiles, less wasteful packaging and less need for labor-saving devices that use up already critically dwindling natural resources.

People are healthier, because they are consuming less poison, getting more exercise, functioning under reduced pressure.

There are fewer heart attacks brought on by insufficient exercise, less cancer caused by pesticide residues and air pollution, fewer nervous disorders brought on by noise pollution.

There are fewer accident victims in hospitals because the murderous automobile-oriented transportation system had been brought under control.

Every product we buy now includes in its price the cost of its ultimate disposal, making many formerly cheap, disposable items so expensive there is no longer a market for them.

Many of the people who once produced these ecology-destroying products are now engaged in a new, creative building industry.

Their main job, as De Bell sees it, is "restructuring the urban waste-lands into planned cities, restoring land to good agricultural uses, building high-quality clustered dwellings at the edges of the good agricultural land using recycled material from the old buildings.

"People ride the short distance to their work and have a chance to farm a little in the sun. There are legs and arms and abdomens where the flab was, and the air is transparent again."

The idea of a steady state would once again be commonplace. The population would be declining to a point where the balance between man and other living things – a balance necessary to man's survival – is being restored.

"The need for and number of schools, doctors, highways, roads, public parks, recreational facilities, swimming pools and other facilities is roughly the same from year to year.

"People work enough to service equipment and to replace things that wear out. They devote energy to increasing the quality of life rather than providing more and more possessions.

"The job of the garbage man and junk man is elevated to the stature of recycling engineer, looping systems in such a way that materials cause no environmental deterioration."

People learn more and more about getting along without gadgets. Ecologically-sound food stores, where you can get pesticide-free produce in returnable containers, prosper.

People have long ago refused to buy ten cents worth of largely synthetic, belly-filling pap in a TV dinner on an aluminum tray that will outlast the food for generations.

Advertising once again serves to inform and not to overstimulate demand or to create useless new demands.

Less wilderness is under pressure from resources industries and more and more redeveloped wilderness is available for public enjoyment.

Poisoning of the ecosystem by leaded automobile gasoline has ceased because redesigned engines no longer require lead additives. The SST (Supersonic transport plane) has long been relegated to the museum where it is viewed with a shudder as a reminder of what might have been if man had not come to his senses.

Mr. De Bell's vision of what might be is undeniably utopian – but the irony is that we may have no choice but to set up such a utopia. Clearly, if we continue on the present path, we are bound for destruction, and sooner than most people realize.

We have already polluted our atmosphere to the extent that some scientists fear we may be on the brink of a new ice age. Smoke and particulate pollutants have so increased the turbidity of the air that less and less solar energy is reaching the earth.

These particles also serve as hitching posts for droplets of moisture which combine to form clouds which further shade the earth from sunshine.

It would only take a very small decrease in the world's mean temperature to bring the glaciers creeping down through Canada and into the central states, the scientists point out.

And they add that careful observations have already shown that mean temperatures around the globe have been falling since 1940.

Other scientists believe that the millions of tons of carbon dioxide poured into the atmosphere each year as a product of combustion in automobiles and industry may be in the process of reversing this trend.

They theorize that the carbon dioxide acts like glass in a greenhouse, trapping heat near the earth's surface, and predict that within a couple of generations temperatures will have risen enough to partially melt the polar ice caps, inundating coastal cities around the globe.

The fact that these two theories directly contradict one another might be cause for a bit of amusing scientist-baiting were it not for the fact that the stakes are so high.

What the two theories do demonstrate is that we are polluting our atmosphere to such an extent that responsible, informed men are convinced that we are altering the world's climatic patterns for all time.

Or take another example of what we are doing to our world.

The United States, in attempting to prepare for huge projected increases in demand for electricity in the coming decades, has moved into a program of wholesale expansion of nuclear power plants.

There are now 15 operable nuclear power plants in the U.S.; 31 more are under construction and a further 56 are planned for the immediate future.

Each of these plants produces huge amounts of radioactive wastes each year, as do the factories which reprocess their spent fuel.

This waste product is millions of times more toxic than any other known industrial pollutant. And it remains highly toxic for hundreds, even thousands of years.

It must be stored carefully, out of harm's reach, virtually forever.

Among the isotopes found in large quantity in the wastes from nuclear plants is strontium 90. One curie of strontium 90 is enough to kill a human.

It is estimated that by the year 2000, the U.S. will have in storage as waste from atomic plants six billion curies of strontium 90. That's 30 times as much as would be released in a major atomic war, or enough to kill every living human twice over.

There are already 75 million gallons of radioactive wastes in storage in the U.S. By 1995, if current trends continue, there will be two billion gallons being stored.

Remember, all of this waste material must be stored *perpetually*. There is no way to decontaminate it.

Remember also that it is so toxic that a few gallons released into a city's water supply could cause havoc measurable only on a scale with nuclear war.

Mankind, needless to say, does not have much experience in building perpetual storage containers. The ones built to date in the U.S. have been plagued with stress and leakage problems, and we are only 25 years into the atomic age.

Logic and mathematics both tell us that sooner or later all of this will add up to an ecological catastrophe, yet the program goes on and Canada, with her abundant reserves of hydroelectric power, joins in with a program of her own that has already spawned two nuclear power plants in Ontario with another planned for Quebec.

Localized pollution problems like mercury poisoning in Canada's inland fisheries and the virtual destruction of Lake Erie, disastrous though they are, seem to pale in comparison with such massive potential calamities.

# You and Pollution

## Frank J. Taylor

Pollution is waste, the accumulation of waste in an unnatural way, with destructive effects on the environment. Affluent men waste; affluent men in quest of greater affluence waste more.

### The Individual

Who pollutes? The individual citizen of developed technological societies pollute. Canadians pollute. Individual attitudes influence social attitudes. These are reflected in all our institutions – business and government. Businessmen and civil servants empowered to make decisions do so based on society's yardsticks. Priorities are changed only by major shifts in power.

Much of the fight against pollution to date has been what M. Dubos has called "palliatives"[1]. Organizations have been formed to fight the "big polluter". The individual considers that his own pollution is insignificant. Affluent society is basically hypocritical. Concern over big wrongs helps to alleviate any personal guilt one might feel for always putting himself first.

The basis of society is the profit motive. We are products of a technologically advanced, free enterprise democracy. In such a system, it is inevitable that some individuals are better at maximizing profits than others. If all desire to profit, then those who profit most must represent an unusual concentration of influence and power. When power is concentrated, institutions are devised to perpetuate it. It should be emphasized that no other technologically developed society has achieved any better results. In communist systems, the state mechanisms of positive and negative inducements to production have produced equally disastrous environmental results. It seems that once technological growth begins, the problem of effluent control increases vastly out of proportion to growth of population.

According to our socio-economic tradition, pollution is normal and natural. If something is done to combat it, then that which is curbed

[1] René Dubos, "The Biosphere," *The UNESCO Courier* (January, 1969), page 13.

will be large scale institutional *over*pollution unless a major shift in personal attitudes takes place.

It would follow, then, that pollution is not a political phenomenon, but one related to human response, magnified through institutions and organizations. It has been pointed out that in North America

> The wastes that besmirch our land are produced in the course of fulfilling widespread human wants that are, in the main, reasonable and defensible.[2]

The car is the largest single air polluter in North America. The motorist is content to blame the auto industry for the inefficiency of his machine, but unwilling to maintain it in peak operating condition. Neither is he willing to give up his personal mobility and explore the feasibility of public transit as an alternative to more and bigger expressways. Public transit is generally desired by the average citizen – for the other fellow to use.

The farmer must be competitive to survive economically. Emphasizing efficiency is his only choice. This means the application of chemical fertilizer, some of which runs off into the rivers and lakes. Nutrient-rich water encourages algae. When algae die they use up oxygen. Eutrification of the water body is the end result. Many chemicals in pesticides and herbicides are new. Their effects on the environment are not fully understood. Only recently has DDT been banned after years of indispensable service on the farm.

Both the farmer and the motorist are innocent individually. They are both pursuing normal, legitimate ends in our society. The majority of Canadians can identify with both situations.

*Government*

In representative government, those who govern must be responsive to the main wants of the voters. The primary objective of the politician is to safeguard his job. Only recently has pollution abatement become a concern. However, there has been no clear indication that the public is prepared to support costly municipal sewage systems with higher taxes. The U.S. politician has an advantage as major public expenditures are brought to the people in plebiscite bond issue votes. This allows government to know where the people stand. The closest Canadian

[2] Max Ways, "How to Think About the Environment," *Fortune* (February, 1970), page 100.

equivalent is public opinion samples. To express great concern costs us nothing. Low priority items are relatively safe from public scrutiny, as the press and the public concentrate on the big expenditures such as education and rapid transit.

The government is therefore able to allot funds to alleviate the troublesome pollution problems, the noticeable ones.

In many Canadian communities government, particularly local government – and, therefore, the people – are the partners of industry. The smaller communities, the resource towns, the larger cities where one industry dominates, are examples. Their presence has meant in some cases prosperity, in others, existence. These very basic facts of life condition attitudes towards that industry. Government in most of these cases has been instrumental in the location of the industry through grants and tax incentives. The smoke rising from chimneys in these towns is a constant source of satisfaction, and reassurance that the future is secure. The individual whose job is represented by the smoke endorses a government policy dedicated to keeping the plant owners free from pressure to respect the surrounding environment. Industry has thus gained a privileged position. The "hands-off" policy of the last half century has not encouraged concern for the environment. "If you want this town to grow it will have to stink."[3] This sentiment aptly illustrates the practical facts of life in struggling communities.

Because of the low priority attached to real conservation, government departments themselves have been directly responsible for discharging effluents into air and water. Provincial and municipal utilities burning high sulphur coal in Toronto spew massive amounts of sulphur dioxide into the air over the city. Municipalities across Canada have been delinquent in municipal sewage treatment. Only recently have towns been coerced into providing this service. Many in Canada still dump wastes directly into streams and lakes. Nor are small cities the only culprits. The St. Lawrence River downstream from Montreal is quite saturated with domestic and industrial pollutants fed into the river from the public sewage system.

One essential difference exists between industry and government – the former can and will pass on the bill for pollution abatement to the consumer through increased prices. The government may even help the private sector through dollar incentives and tax exemptions. At some

[3] Sanford Rose, "The Economics of Environmental Quality," *Fortune* (February, 1970), page 120.

level, usually provincial, government must pay its own bill. The same public that accepts a price rise as an annual inevitability is not nearly as understanding about yearly tax increases. The worth of a politician is often measured by his ability to prevent tax increases despite a louder public plea for more and better services. It would seem that the piper does call the tune. For some time the refrain has been anachronistic.

## Industry

Manufacturers are admittedly responsible for a large part of the ecological destruction. Although the damage is done in the processing plants it is the corporate boardrooms that are primarily responsible. It is here where the policy decisions are made, where the individuals responsible for these decisions can choose between an extra few cents per share in earnings, and increased costs for abatement equipment. It is here where promotion and advertising departments design their assaults on the gullible public.

Business is geared to profit. The first responsibility is to the shareholder. The individuals that make up the system are therefore programmed to think in terms of success being equal to dollars earned for the company. Promotion depends on it, salary depends on it, *ad infinitum.*

> The competitive market system is rigged against conservation. The effect of omitting free resources from the pricing system is to make the economy as a whole pay a huge subsidy to those activities that put above average pressure on free resources. In short we are now providing a huge unintentional market incentive to pollution.[4]

Organized labour puts pressure on prices; rising costs for extraction and delivery of raw materials put pressure on prices; higher costs of building and development add their pressures. To remain competitive, manufacturers must utilize technology – also at great expense. There is comparatively little pressure to guarantee pure water and air. By installing pollution control devices the manufacturer is adding, for the most part, dead cost with little chance of recovery. Costs related to fouled air and water are borne by other manufacturers or by the public. When some competitors do not invest in pollution control, those who do are forced to compete unfairly. When one industry pollutes as a means of

[4] Max Ways, *op cit*, page 160.

economizing, its cost structure is artifically low. Another industry may have to spend money to treat the polluted water before it can use it. If this is the case then the second industry is subsidizing the lower costs of the first. The individual will unwittingly reward the culprit by purchasing his cheaper product.

In North America, resources have been abundant and cheap. Land, minerals, labour have all acquired a market value in goods production. Air and water are still largely excluded from the pricing system, both as raw materials, and as disposal media.

Equally important to business is the necessity to convince people to buy, to trade-in the old or to discard a good in favour of the new improved model. This has resulted in "pervasive throw-away psychology". In its drive for the new and different, technology is not geared to recycling wastes but rather to encourage waste. No better example of this psychology can be found than the case of the non-returnable bottle. The idea of "throw-away" containers was used for sales promotion. So successful was the campaign that it is difficult to walk through any public place without seeing its legacy. The returnable bottle, a recycled container, became a "casualty of affluence". The further impact of a packaging revolution can be seen in any supermarket. Sales promotion and ease of handling dictate the necessity to package packaged things together in packages.

The businessman is applying the yardsticks of a society that is motivated by the same goal. Boardroom philosophy is conditioned by the knowledge that the man on the street is primarily interested in maximizing personal profit.

The rapid evolution of technology has not helped affluent man, rather it has tended to accelerate destruction. In business and in government, rapid technological growth has led to specialization, which in turn has created fragmented departments, each with its own budget, responsibilities and goals. Communication is minimal. Research has been directed towards the solution of specific problems relating to individual, narrowly defined aims. Specialization in society has created the technocrat and the bureaucrat. The technocrat narrows the problem and finds new solutions, thereby increasing the chances of new side-effects. But this is no great concern because the bureaucrat will create a special department to deal with the side-effects. Research is expensive. The profit motive in industry and the tight budget in government dictate the least cost solution as necessary or practical. For example, the fact that a new product may create other problems by its use or in being discarded cannot be considered. In the same way, the city builds an express-way or clears a slum. Problem solved?

## Conservation

The situation today is reflected in the dilemma facing the conservation-ist. For a long time naturalists and conservationists were alone in their concern for the man-centred ecosystem. Dasmond, writing in *The Destruction of California* feels that

> Conservation . . . today is often a piecemeal, stopgap activity that is often too late, and usually too little. It stands too often in the path of what is called progress, and thus arouses the ire of those concerned with moneymaking. Conservationists find themselves always in the desperate position of trying to impose some control over an activity that is already underway, or of trying to save some piece of land or scenery against the opposition of powerful pressure groups. Always their activities seem beside the point to those involved in the main business of our society.[5]

In sum, concern for the environment has been secondary, peripheral and impractical.

> In every aspect of life there is a tendency not to see, hear, feel, or think – this often is the result of conditioning. There is little recognition of cause and effect – so attempts are made to solve a problem without attacking the basic cause. There is little con-cern for problems even when they are recognized, unless they affect the individual personally.
> Under existing conditions if standards were set by cultural tolerance alone, they would be abysmally low. In fact they are. Where scientist and philosopher are concerned by problems of pollution, the general public either does not recognize the state of the environment as being polluted, cannot appreciate the consequences, or is apathetic.[6]

## Where From Here

There would seem to be several alternatives. One would be to accept the suggestion of the preceding article, return to the "good old days" –

[5] R. Dasmond, *The Destruction of California* (New York, Macmillan, 1968), page 187.
[6] H. P. and B. L. Van Ginkel, "The Phenomenon of Pollution," *The Pollution Reader* (Montreal, Harvest House, 1968), page 16.

reject technology, bring back self-sufficiency. A corollary would be to arbitrarily halt technological growth at the present level, selecting only desirable areas for expansion. No matter how appealing and simple this solution may seem it must be rejected on the grounds that affluent man is confident in his ability to use technology to reverse the destructive tendency of his society. Nor will we

> Improve our environmental situation by recommending a technological retreat on the basis of what each of us considers the superfluous items in the household of his neighbours.[7]

A society whose technology, attitudes and institutions created the environmental crisis can solve it. Positive results have been achieved now in arousing the public, combatting apathy and illustrating that there is some understanding of cause and effect, that some do care and that some have discovered the use of the media to bring pressure for fundamental reform. Unfortunately, considerable emphasis must be placed on the word *some*. Numbers are growing, particularly in the informed sections of society. DDT, phosphates and mercury are representative victories.

Business and government have the necessary resources to effect real change. Despite the fact that society stresses individuality, few would argue against the necessity for a restraining force or for positive leadership. Business and the public expect government to establish the bounds within which competitive enterprise functions. Similarly, it is expected that government will set an example at all levels. Government can illustrate the use of inter-disciplinary expertise in problem solving; the use of public involvement in planning, through rearranged, integrated departments.

New legislation is necessary to reallocate the burden of costs for damages done to the ecosystem, and to stimulate the private sector to make more effort in pollution technology. Air and water are resources. They can be recycled in the production process. As resources they have a value and must be paid for when used. Taxes related to the volume and undesirability of pollutants introduced into air and water must be levied. The result would be that the goods produced by negligent manufacturers will bear a higher price tag on the market place. Public selection will then operate against them, forcing expenditure on pollution abatement. In order to discourage the continued development of items that cause

[7] Max Ways, *op cit*, page 101.

environmental problems after sale or consumption, a disposal tax could be levied.

The end result should be a combination of the consumer, government and industry applying pressure to solve pollution problems. The consumer is price conscious and will not pay a premium to support polluters. Industry is cost conscious and is public relations conscious. As long as individuals have more pressure on the government than industry, the people will force government to allow them to select the virtuous in the market place.

The business community itself has begun to take advantage of rising public concern. Initiative in creating and advertising low pollution items has proven profitable in some sectors. This indicates a promising beginning in the reallocation of resources, which may have far reaching results.

The ultimate outcome must remain in doubt. The problem arose mainly through negligence, failure to see the end results of personal and collective actions motivated by a desire for affluence. While the individual professes concern for pollution, this is no guarantee that he himself will cease to pollute or in fact realize that he is a polluter. To most, pollution means the factory and the power plant – not their car, faulty septic tank, or backyard fire. It is a question of scale. If man continues to rationalize his personal position and contribution to the problem, then no fundamental change in thinking will occur. The same attitudes are defensible on a larger scale. Real solution will have escaped us!

# Man the Modifier

Section

# 2

*Suicide is incomprehensible to Man, under ordinary conditions. Yet Man is apparently unconcerned with his progress towards race suicide. Conservationists give Man a very limited time before a major calamity will end society as we know it. Fortunately, some authorities and citizens are taking action in attempts to stop humanicide.*

*Section 2 expands on the first part of the book by indicating specific areas in which the balance of the spaceship is being upset.*

*Part A deals with air pollution. Philip Leighton's article,* Geographical Aspects of Air Pollution *discusses the situation in Los Angeles – perhaps the best (or worst) geographical setting for a study of air pollution problems. The writing, and the problems, belong to a specific location. However, many of the concepts, ideas, conclusions, and much of the information, are applicable to Canadian urban areas.*

*Faltermayer, in* We Can Afford Clean Air, *indicates how economics affect the situation, and how much the remedies might cost.*

*Part B shows, as clearly as any, how complex is the problem. Many interests are at work. Some of the opinions expressed run completely counter to others. An attempt has been made to give as broad a coverage as possible. As can be seen, there is rarely a simple solution.*

*The polluting of our soil, both by chemical and mechanical means, is discussed in Part C. Particularly interesting are the twists of politics expressed in* Pitfalls in New Mining Plans.

*The pesticide dilemma is expanded in Part D. The DDT controversy is still a very active one. The article* Mysterious Pollution: The Green Infection *shows how delicate some ecological balances can be.*

*Part E looks at the "throw-away society", and how better use could be made of our wasted resources.*

*The noise pollution situation is examined in Part F, and* The Deafening Din *gives some rather alarming statistics.*

# Part A

# The Limitless Sky

# Only Pressure
# Will Do It

Launching an information program on pollution is a laudable undertaking, and a good many listeners probably nodded agreement with Premier John Robarts when he admitted: "I don't think I want to face my grandchildren at some stage of the game and have to answer their question: 'What went wrong?' " Even if the prospect of accounting for one's shortcomings to his grandchildren may hold out sufficient inducement to prod any reasonable person into action, we would suggest to Mr. Robarts that time may not be on his side. It may already be too late to avoid those questions.

It is going to require much more than public information programs if the threat which Mr. Robarts himself describes as "devastating" is to be met. The Premier, however, couldn't seem to resolve the dilemma posed by the alternatives he outlined. To force companies to discontinue practices which "until recently were acceptable, or at least tolerated" would involve "enormous costs, disrupt industry, cause large-scale unemployment and be excessively unfair and harsh". He admits, however, that the effect these practices are having on environment cannot be allowed to continue.

Mr. Robarts is trying to balance short-run costs against long-term effects and it is the kind of equation that will never balance. Mr. Robarts, his Government, and the other levels of government involved really have no choice in the matter. The pulp and paper company which is polluting the water it uses and the chemical company which is polluting the atmosphere have the responsibility for correcting the damage they have done. Of course, the governments can help but they also have the responsibility to see that the corrective measures are undertaken with some dispatch.

Mr. Robarts described as "a new and large step forward in the battle against pollution" the concentrating "all environment management control activities within the Department of Energy and Resources Management". This is only the baby step forward. George Kerr, minister for this department, points with some pride at the $1,000 fine recently levied against Domtar Ltd. on a charge laid by the Ontario Water Resources Commission at Nipigon Bay.

Thousand-dollar fines for large corporations amount to little more than the licensing proposal put forward by Mr. Kerr's federal colleague, Energy Resources Minister J. J. Greene. Tough and co-ordinated action – on government, not industry's timetable – is what now must be forthcoming from Mr. Kerr and Mr. Robarts.

# Geographical Aspects of Air Pollution

## Philip A. Leighton

*. . . this most excellent canopy, the air, look you, this brave o'erhanging firmament, this majestical roof fretted with golden fire, why, it appears no other things to me than a foul and pestilent congregation of vapours.*

– Hamlet, Act II, Scene ii.

It is reasonable to suppose that man originally evolved with few if any inhibitions regarding the use of that part of his environment which he was able to capture and hold from his competitors. Only with experience, as his knowledge and numbers increased, did he come to realize that the physical requirements of life are limited and that their use must be regulated. Since earliest history he has been devising systems for the ownership, protection, and use of land and food, and, more recently, of water. Last of all to become subject to this realization and regulation is air. Here the tradition of free use is still dominant. We respect rights of ownership in land, food, and water, but except as a medium of transportation we recognize none for air.

Curiously, this divergence in attitude, or in the stage of modification of attitude, does not parallel either the urgency of man's needs or his ability to adapt his surroundings to meet those needs. He can live indefinitely away from land, he can go several weeks without food and several days without water, awake he normally eats and drinks only at intervals, and asleep he does neither, but awake or asleep his need for air is never further away than his next breath. As for ability to adapt, he can when he so wishes improve the land, he can improve and transport food and water, but except on a small scale, as in air conditioning in dwellings and other buildings or the use of wind machines in orchards, he cannot yet improve or transport air. Outdoor air in the main he only contaminates.

As a result of such prodigal uses of air for waste disposal, the employment of technology has contributed far more to the production of air pollution than to its abatement, and it is clear that the ratio must be reversed if man as a breathing organism is to keep a suitable environment. But to define the extent to which the uses of air must be regulated, we must first know something about how much is available. As with man's other needs, it is a simple matter of supply and demand.

## The Supply of Air

The height of the troposphere in the middle latitudes, 10–14 km, is about one five-hundredth of the earth's radius. This is a thin skin indeed, yet it contains about four-fifths of all the air in the atmosphere, and to man on the surface of the earth the layer of air available for waste disposal is usually only a fraction – and sometimes only a very small fraction – of the troposphere. The air supply at the surface is limited to an extent that varies with place and time, and the factors contributing to the limited surface ventilation are both meteorological and topographic.

The most common meteorological factors are inversions that limit vertical mixing of air and low winds that limit its lateral transport. An inversion is a decrease in air temperature with increasing altitude above the surface, which for the United States and international standard atmospheres is 0.65° C per 100 meters (Figure 1). A parcel of air ascending in the atmosphere expands with the decreasing pressure and is thereby cooled, and when this process occurs adiabatically, the rate of cooling, or the adiabatic lapse rate, in unsaturated air is about 1° C per 100 meters. When the atmospheric lapse rate is less than this, as it is in the standard atmosphere, an ascending air parcel becomes cooler, and hence denser, than the surrounding air, and work is required to lift it against the downward force produced by the density difference. Similarly, a parcel of air being lowered in a subadiabatic temperature gradient becomes warmer and less dense than the surrounding air,

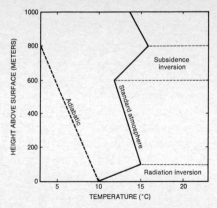

Figure 1. *Temperature profile through two inversion layers.*

producing an upward force against which work is again required. When the temperature gradient is inverted, the amount of work required to move a parcel of air across the inversion layer usually exceeds the supply

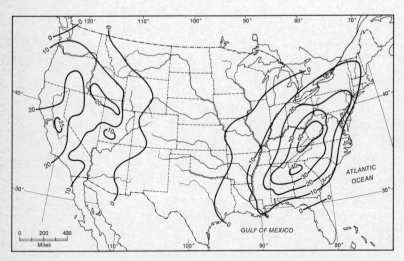

Figure 2. *The air pollution potential advisory forecasts of the Division of Air Pollution, United States Public Health Service, began August 1, 1960, for the eastern United States, and October 1, 1963, for the western United States. The numbers shown on the contours indicate the number of forecast days from the initiation date in each case through December, 1964. Source: data from R. A. McCormick.*

available through turbulence and other atmospheric processes, and there is, in consequence, little or no mixing through the layer.

Inversions occur both at the surface and aloft. Surface inversions are most commonly produced by cooling of the ground by radiation loss, which in turn cools the surface air, and their depth, intensity, and duration are determined by the wind velocity, the nature of the surface, the transparency of the air above the surface to the emitted radiation, and the amount of solar radiation during the following day. The chief absorbers, in air, of the long-wave infra-red emitted by a surface at ordinary temperatures are water and carbon dioxide. Hence radiative

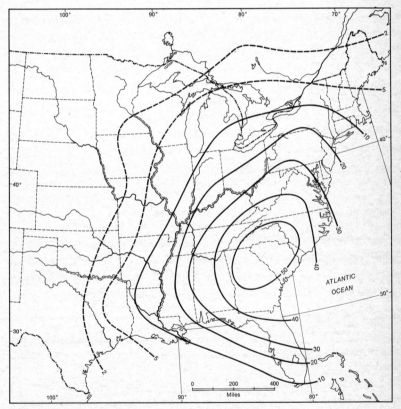

Figure 3. *Number of periods in which stagnating high-pressure cells produced low winds for four or more successive days in the eastern United States, 1936–1956. Source: J. Korshover.*

cooling is most marked when the air is dry and pure, and it increases with altitude as the amount of air overhead is reduced.

The commonest source of inversions aloft is the subsidence that normally accompanies high-pressure systems, but overhead inversions may also be produced, both on a local scale and on an air-mass or frontal scale, by the intrusion of cold air under warm or by the over-running of cold air by warm. In the middle latitudes subsidence inversions are most marked in the anticyclonic gradients on the easterly sides of high-pressure cells and approach closer to the surface with increasing distance from the cell center. For this reason the west coasts of the continents are subject to relatively low overhead inversions from the semipermanent marine highs, and these inversions may last for many days. Along the Southern California coast, for example, inversions below 762 m (2500 ft), mostly due to subsidence associated with the Pacific high, exist 90 percent or more of the time during the summer months.

*Topographic Effects*

Perhaps the most important effects of topography in limiting the supply of surface air are produced by drainage. Just as water drains down slopes and gullies to form rivers in valleys and lakes in basins, so the air, cooled by radiation loss, drains down those slopes at night. And like flowing water, these density or gravity flows of cold air tend to follow regular channels, which may be marked out almost as definitely as the course of a stream. The volume of air drainage, however, is much larger than that of water drainage; hence the aircourses are broader, and if the valley or basin is not too wide the flows soon collect to reach across it. The layers thus formed, further cooled by radiation loss in the valley or basin itself, become so stable that they often completely control the surface wind direction and velocity and thus control the air supply; the gradient wind is blocked out, and even the gravity flows from the surrounding slopes tend to overrun the air in the bottom (Figure 4). After sunrise thermal upslope flow soon sets in on slopes exposed to the sun, but gravity flow may continue until late morning on shady slopes, and even all day on steep northern slopes.

The cold layers accumulated by this process during the long nights of winter may become so deep, with inversions so intense, that they are not broken up by insolation during the short days; and when this happens, severely limited ventilation will persist until a change in weather produces gradient winds high enough, or a cold wedge strong enough, to

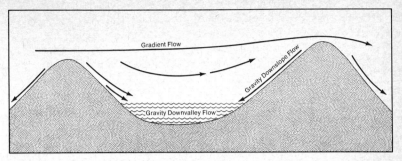

Figure 4. *In the case diagrammed, the gradient wind is blocked out of the valley by the bordering mountains, and the air supply on the valley floor is limited to that in the lower part of the gravity downvalley flow.*

sweep out the valley or basin. For any particular combination of topography there is usually a wind velocity below which the local flows are dominant and above which the gradient wind is dominant. The smaller the relief, the lower is this critical velocity; for relief differences of 300–600 m it is of the order of 10–15 knots.

In coastal areas, warming and cooling of the land, while the water temperature remains fairly constant, produce the familiar pattern of land–sea breezes, which are usually thought of as improving ventilation but which may under certain circumstances restrict it. An example is found in the Los Angeles basin, where the Santa Monica Mountains to the northwest and the Sierra Madre to the north furnish shelter to the extent that local airflow is usually dominant under the subsidence inversion. This local flow consists chiefly of a gentle seaward drainage at night and a more rapid landward movement by day. But the mountains rising above the inversion layer retard the sweeping out of the basin by the landward movement, and the diurnal reversal in direction tends to move air back and forth in the basin. As a result of this entrapment, there is often some carry-over of pollutants from the day before, and pollutants emitted at night move toward or out over the sea, only to be swept back over the land the next morning. On occasion this polluted air is carried back over a neighboring area, even a fairly distant one; thus eye irritation came to Santa Barbara for the first time in January, 1965, partly as the result of this process.

These effects are enhanced by a cold upwelling in the ocean along most of the California coast, which produces surface-water temperatures lower than the temperatures farther out to sea. As the surface

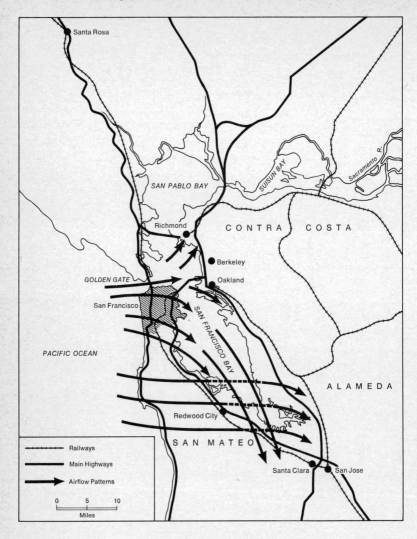

Figure 5. *Daytime airflow patterns in the San Francisco Bay area.*
*In the southern part of the Bay area, wind coming over the mountains to*
*the west overrides the colder air coming down the bay, producing an*
*overhead inversion that may contribute to the severity of air pollution in*
*the Palo Alto–San Jose area.*

layer of air moves over this cold water it also is cooled. One result is the familiar coastal fog of California, but a more important result, with respect to air pollution, is the additional stability the cooling imparts to the landward-moving air.

The airflow patterns in the San Francisco Bay Area illustrate another mechanism by which water may limit the air supply. During the extensive season of the semipermanent Pacific high, air cooled by the offshore ocean upwelling flows through the Golden Gate and between the hills of San Francisco to the inner bay (Figure 5). Part of this air crosses the bay and is deflected to the north and south by the east-bay hills, and part travels south and southeast over the bay itself. Meanwhile, another flow of air reaches the south-bay area by moving inland across the mountains to the west. This air, having traveled farther over land, is warmer than the air that comes down the bay, and when the two flows intersect, the warmer overrides the cooler and produces a local overhead inversion that around Palo Alto may be less than 100 m above the ground. Although the existence of this effect was demonstrated twenty years ago, its contribution to the severity of air pollution in the south-bay area remains to be determined.

As urbanization and industrialization expand over the world it is interesting, and possibly beneficial, to attempt some assessment of the local air supply in areas that are still relatively empty. Although aerogeographical surveys would be required for an adequate assessment, tentative indications may be obtained merely by consulting maps and weather data. For instance, topography alone suggests that the Granby basin in Colorado would be a poor location in which to build a smelter, and both topography and weather data suggest that such places as the Santa Ynez valley in California and the Sous plain in Morocco should certainly be surveyed before any large industrial or urban development is undertaken. But one does not have to go far in this search to find that most of the unfavorable locations are already occupied. The factors that limit local ventilation are also factors conducive to habitation, and it is ironic that the areas of the world in which the air supply is on occasion most limited are often the areas in which man has chosen to build his cities.

Fortunately, poor ventilation, whether produced by general inversions and low winds or by local conditions, does not exist all the time. The sparkling clarity still enjoyed on days of good ventilation, even over large urban areas, serves to emphasize the great effect of limited air

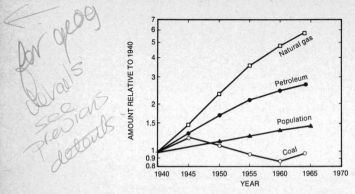

Figure 6. *Changes in the fossil fuel consumption in the United States.*

supply on the poor days, and the extent to which it increases the problems of air pollution.

## Increase of Photochemical Air Pollution

A more difficult group of problems, most of which remain for future solution, arise when the sources of pollution, although specific, are not fixed or for other reasons cannot be easily controlled. In this category are such things as agricultural dust, smoke from agricultural burning, airborne insecticides, and hydrogen sulphide and other obnoxious gases from sewage and organic industrial wastes.

Not all the hydrocarbons emitted to the air take part in the photochemical* reactions. Methane, the chief component of natural gas, is inactive. Acetylene, benzene, and the simple paraffins such as propane and butane are nearly inactive. On the other hand, all the olefins, the more complex aromatics, and the higher paraffins are reactive, though they differ widely both in rate and in products. These reactive hydrocarbons come from motor vehicles, from the production, refining, and marketing of petroleum and petroleum products, and from the evaporation of solvents. Other emissions that may play some part in photochemical air pollution are aldehydes, which come chiefly from the incomplete combustion of organic materials, and sulphur dioxide. When these emissions are mixed, diluted in air, and exposed to sunlight, they undergo photochemical reactions that lead to the conversion of the nitric oxide to nitrogen dioxide, which has a brown color and may have

---

* A photochemical reaction is one that requires a source of light (in this case, sunlight) in order to take place.

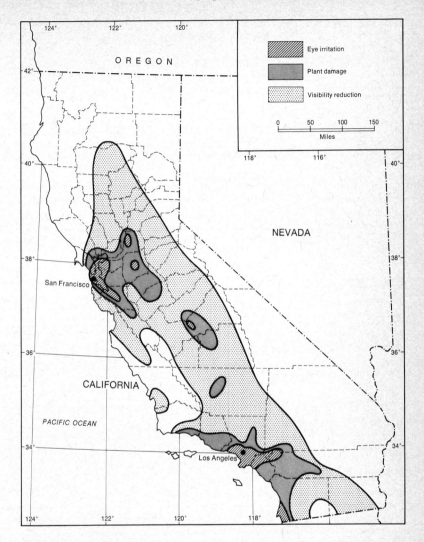

Figure 7. *Extent of general air pollution in California, 1961–1963. The plant damage areas are specific, but the eye irritation and visibility reduction may be due in part to forms of general air pollution other than photochemical. Sources: for plant damage, J. T. Middleton: California against Air Pollution (California Department of Public Health, Sacramento, 1961); for eye irritation and visibility reduction, local reports and personal observations up to December, 1963.*

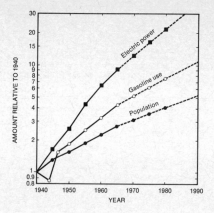

Figure 8. *With the exception of the war years, the increase in gasoline use and, to a smaller extent, that of electric power generation relative to population, have followed the exponential relation* $A/A_{1940} = P/P_{1940}{}^{n}$, *where* $A/A_{1940}$ *is the amount of gasoline use or power production relative to 1940 and* $P/P_{1940}$ *is the corresponding ratio for population. The indicated average values of* n *are 1.5 for gasoline use and about 2.2 for electric power, and the projections were made on this basis. Source: population projection to 1980, Financial and Population Research Section, California State Department of Finance.*

adverse effects on plants and animals if its concentration becomes high enough. This is followed, and sometimes accompanied, by the formation of particulates that reduce visibility, of ozone and peroxyacyl nitrates (PAN) that damage plants, and of formaldehyde and other products that, along with the peroxyacyl nitrates, cause eye irritation.

An increasing intensity of pollution is required to produce these symptoms of photochemical air pollution, lowest for visibility reduction, intermediate for plant damage, and highest for eye irritation.

This remarkable spread may be traced to two factors, the first of which is that nitrogen oxide and hydrocarbon emissions have increased faster than the population. The largest source of both nitrogen oxides and hydrocarbons is the automobile; in California at the present time about 60 percent of the nitrogen oxides and 75 to 85 percent of the reactive hydrocarbons, depending on how these are estimated, come from motor vehicles. Between 1940 and 1965 the population of California increased 2.7 times and gasoline use by motor vehicles in the state

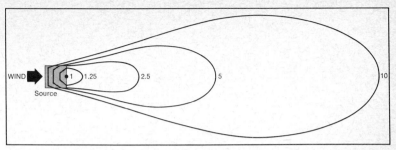

Figure 9. *Area coverage by a pollutant as a function of emission rate. The figures are relative emission rates, and the curves are the corresponding isopleths of given concentration. Estimated for a uniform square source with constant wind direction and speed under an overhead inversion at a constant height.*

increased 4.3 times (Figure 8). The growth in electric-power generation, now 9.2 times what it was in 1940, has been another contributor to increasing nitrogen oxide emissions; roughly 16 percent of the present nitrogen oxide emissions in California come from steam-electric power plants. Hydrocarbon emissions, on the other hand, over the state as a whole have probably increased more in accordance with gasoline use.

The second factor contributing to the growth of photochemical air pollution is the relation between emission rate and the area covered by a given concentration as the pollutants are carried by the wind. This may be illustrated, for idealized conditions, by use of the box model, which assumes uniform mixing to a constant height such as an overhead inversion base, with dilution by lateral diffusion beneath that ceiling. The isopleths for a given concentration, calculated from this model for various emission rates in a uniform square source (that is, an idealized city), under constant wind direction and velocity are shown in Figure 9. Starting, by definition, with the given concentration appearing at only a single point when the emission rate is unity, the areas within the isopleths are seen to increase much faster than the corresponding emission rates.

When a specific symptom of pollution has expanded to fill a geographical area, as is the case with plant damage in the Los Angeles basin and the San Francisco Bay Area, further increase may be expected to be in intensity rather than in extent. However, the movement of pollutants from one airshed to another is not excluded (Figure 7); the fingers of plant damage extending north and east from the Los Angeles region and southeast and east from the Bay region show that these areas are still growing, and if photochemical air pollution is not abated it may be assumed that the present visibility-reduction area is a shadow of the coming plant-damage area, and the present plant-damage area a forecast of the coming eye-irritation area.

## The Prospects for Control

Although photochemical air pollution is well on its way to becoming the number one form of general air pollution in the United States, a broad attack against it has thus far been mounted only in California. However, the passage by Congress on October 1, 1965, of a bill requiring the installation after September, 1967, of exhaust control devices on new automobiles of domestic manufacture will expand this attack to a national scale, and in view of this prospect the California program merits examination in some detail.

In an assessment of the prospects for the abatement of photochemical air pollution by automobile controls, three factors are pertinent: the time delay or lead time; the growth in emissions over that lead time; and the degree of control likely to be achieved. To go back in time, we may now say that the visibility reduction which had become widespread in the Los Angeles basin as early as 1920 was due, in part at least, to photochemical air pollution. Reduction in the sizes of oranges and the cracking of rubber products, now known to be due to photochemical air pollution, were reported at least as early as 1930, specific plant damage was first observed in 1942, and eye irritation had appeared by 1945. The first step toward control was taken in 1948 with a California legislative act establishing air pollution control districts, and the control program in Los Angeles County was initiated shortly thereafter. Not until 1952 was the first evidence obtained that what was then known as "smog" was primarily photochemical and that the emissions chiefly responsible for it were nitrogen oxides and hydrocarbons.

The first control steps directed specifically at photochemical air pollution were applied to hydrocarbon emissions from stationary sources in the Los Angeles basin, and by 1960 these sources were about 60 percent controlled. In 1957–1958 the elimination of home incinerators and the restriction of fuel-oil burning during the smog season achieved about a 45 percent control of nitrogen oxide emissions from stationary sources in the basin. The attack on hydrocarbon emissions from motor vehicles was initiated on a statewide basis in 1959. Roughly 75–80 percent of the reactive hydrocarbons emitted by automobiles come from the exhaust, 14–17 percent from the crankcase, and 7–8 percent from carburetor and

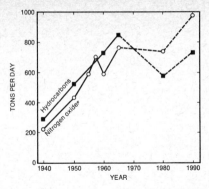

Figure 10. *The projections assume that the population predictions of the California State Department of Finance will be realized; that emissions will continue to increase relative to population as they have since 1940; that motor vehicle crankcase emissions will be 80 per cent controlled, exhaust and evaporation hydrocarbons 70 per cent controlled, and exhaust nitrogen oxides 60 per cent controlled by 1980; and that no other controls will be adopted. Source: for emissions to 1965, P. A. Leighton.*

fuel-tank evaporation. Installation of crank-case control devices on new cars began in 1961, but their installation on used cars has encountered complex difficulties and delays. Moreover, experience has shown that in the hands of individual owners the actual control achieved by these devices falls considerably short of the theoretical, and judgments of the degree of crankcase hydrocarbon control that will eventually be achieved range from less than 70 percent to about 90 percent.

A standard for exhaust hydrocarbons and carbon monoxide, which specifies that the hydrocarbon content under a given cycle of operation shall not exceed an average of 275 ppm, was adopted in 1960, and the installation on new automobiles of devices intended to meet this standard is beginning with the 1966 models of domestic makes. Revised standards now scheduled to take effect in 1970 will reduce the allowed exhaust hydrocarbon content to 180 ppm and will also require a reduction in evaporation losses. If the installation of devices to meet these 1970 standards is limited to new cars it will be at least 1980 before the exhaust control program as it now stands is fully effective, and judgments of the degree of exhaust hydrocarbon control that may be achieved range from 50 percent to 80 percent, the latter being the theoretical value. A standard of 350 ppm for exhaust nitrogen oxides, which is now in process of adoption, will require devices that produce a theoretical 65 percent control of these emissions.

What this attack has accomplished and may be expected to accomplish must be assessed in relation to the growth in sources and emissions that has occurred and may be expected over the time periods concerned. An assessment on this basis for Los Angeles County is shown in Figure 10. Examination of the hydrocarbon curve indicates that neither the controls of emissions from stationary sources initiated after 1950 nor the crankcase controls initiated in 1961 have been sufficient to counteract the overall increase in emissions that accompanied population growth in the county. It would appear that the automobile exhaust and evaporation controls now scheduled will indeed reduce hydrocarbon emissions, even in the face of prospective growth, but if no further steps are taken, the upward climb will be resumed after the program is completed. According to the nitrogen oxide curve the controls of stationary sources initiated in 1957–1958 achieved some reduction, but by about 1963 the gains had been wiped out by the process of growth. The projection indicates that the prospective control of nitrogen oxides from motor vehicles will reduce the overall emissions slightly between 1965 and 1980, but the growth after 1980, if no further steps are taken, will soon carry these emissions to new highs.

In essence these ultimate problems of general air pollution may be stated in simple terms. Whether applied to a local area or to the entire atmosphere it is a matter of maintaining the relation

$$\frac{\text{Emissions per capita} \times \text{number of persons}}{\text{Air supply}} < X,$$

where $X$ is the maximum value that we can accommodate. The means of maintaining this relation, however, are another matter. There is little prospect of increasing the local supply of air and none of increasing the overall supply. The per capita emissions may be reduced by controls, but, as we have seen, with increasing population the steps required become successively more severe, and the end of the process is the elimination of the sources. The accommodation coefficient $X$, as far as direct physiological effects are concerned, could be increased by the use of protective methods through which we breathed only purified air, but this would not help unprotected life forms or retard the other effects that must be taken into account. The remaining factor in the equation is

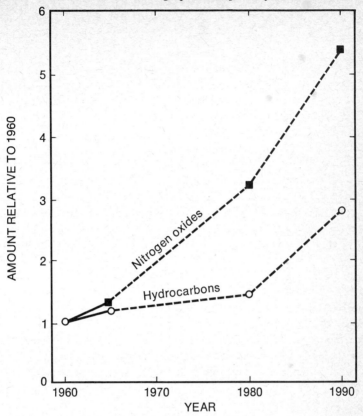

Figure 11. *The projections assume that hydrocarbon emissions before controls will increase with gasoline use; that nitrogen oxide emissions from stationary sources will triple between 1965 and 1980 and will increase with population between 1980 and 1990; that vehicular nitrogen oxides will increase with gasoline use to the 1.1 power, and that the controls applied will be the same as in Figure 10.*

the number of persons, and it may well be that the resource which eventually forces man to adopt population control as a requirement for survival will not be land, food, or water, but air.

When these factors and the predicted population increase are taken into account, the projections in Figure 11 indicate that the present California motor-vehicle control program in itself will not be sufficient to arrest the growth of photochemical pollution in the Salinas Valley.

*Industry and the automobile are easily singled out as air polluters. Often forgotten in the smog are public utilities, schools, office buildings and private houses, which make use of low grade bunker oil or soft coal. These two power and heat sources emit large amounts of $SO_2$ and ash.* Polluters or Not: It Depends on the Fuel *offers a reason for the use of natural gas as a fuel.*

# Polluters or Not?
# Depends on the Fuel

Are public utilities guilty of pollution? Sometimes. Much depends, of course, on the utility's source of power. If it's natural gas as in British Columbia then the problem is minimal.

In Ontario, the use of coal to produce power has earned Ontario Hydro much criticism from anti-pollution groups.

Under fire is the coal-burning Lakeshore generating plant owned by Ontario Hydro, west of Toronto. Some pollution groups, notably Pollution Probe in Toronto, recently held an inquiry into the continued smoke pollution from the plant's four chimneys.

Ontario's Richard L. Hearn Station in Metropolitan Toronto is also a coal burner with eight chimneys belching out sulphur dioxide. These chimneys are to be replaced by a single 750-foot-high stack that will help spread the offending gas over as wide an area as possible.

"We do not pretend it is a perfect solution – or a solution for all time," says George Gathercole, Ontario Hydro chairman.

"No perfect answer is available. You cannot burn coal in the quantities we do, nor can society as a whole use fossil fuels on the scale it does for household and other heating, transportation, and industrial processes, and hope to achieve pristine pure air.

"We are confident that this stack offers an effective and practical solution to this specific problem. We are backing up this confidence with a willingness to spend nearly $9 million."

Halifax Mayor Allan O'Brien says there have been some complaints

*Richard L. Hearn Generating Station, Toronto.*

about air pollution caused by Nova Scotia Light & Power's two coal-burning power plants in the city.

One major incident in recent years occurred when a malfunction in the company's equipment allowed an excess amount of soot to escape.

Manitoba's two power utilities so far have clean bills of health.

L. A. Kay, vice-chairman and secretary of the province's Clean Environment Commission, says:

"Our laws concerning pollution are a little different to other provinces. If we find a public utility discharging too many solids, they have to apply for an interim license to continue. The Commission can continue the interim license for a period up to five years."

This policy was adopted so utilities and industries would not be forced to take drastic and costly action on short notice. However, the commission does have authority to take swift action if it uncovers a serious problem.

The only action the commission has taken was to ask Winnipeg

Hydro, the city-owned power utility, to apply for an interim license to continue using its downtown steam-heating plant, which is a coal burner. The plant belches smoke during the winter months and Winnipeg Hydro officials suspect they will have to make revisions to the plant to reduce the relatively small amount of air pollution involved.

Alberta's electric and natural gas utilities are not major contributors to that province's air and water pollution problems. The reasons:

With exceptions (notably Edmonton, Medicine Hat and Lethbridge which operate their own generating plants), all electric power production is carried out in remote areas and employs fuels which, according to industry and provincial government officials, do not figure in the urban pollution problem.

The province's largest electric utility – Calgary Power Ltd. – generates most of its base load in a single, coal-fired thermal power complex on Lake Wabamun, about 40 miles west of Edmonton.

Similarly, the province's other major investor-owned electric utility – Canadian Utilities Ltd. – also relies largely on coal-fired thermal production for its output. Its major generating facility is also located in a relatively underpopulated area at Forestburg, on the Battle River, about 80 miles southeast of Edmonton.

These two plants, which between them produce an estimated 60% of the province's present base load requirement, are fueled by a type of coal (low in sulphur) which produces a negligible amount of pollutants.

Alberta's only truly major, urban-area power generating facility is Edmonton Power's 392,000 kilowatt thermal generating plant, in that city's mid-town Rossdale Flats area.

However, both municipal and utility sources say the plant is not a polluter. Responding to provincial government complaints initiated several years ago, Edmonton Power – the municipally owned generating/distribution facility – invested nearly $500,000 in pollution control equipment (items included an addition to a major smokestack) and both municipal and provincial government studies indicate that the plant is no longer suspect.

Equally clean in the eyes of Alberta's pollution sleuths are the province's two major gas distributing organizations – Canadian Western Natural Gas Co., Calgary, and Northwestern Utilities Ltd., Edmonton, wholesalers/retailers of processed natural gas. They do not have gas processing plants of their own.

Quebec has few of the pollution problems besetting other provinces more dependent on non-hydraulic methods of power generation.

*Air Pollution causes 50% of all human diseases. Sensationalist? Stop and consider. Cancer has been shown to be caused by smoke. The actual breathing of pollutants is a disease starter. But particles diffused in the air reduce the amount of sunlight reaching the earth. We seldom consider the effects of this. It has been suggested that Rickets, long thought to be caused by Vitamin D deficiency, may be a result of lack of sunlight, which the body needs to absorb the Vitamin.*

*More particles in the air results in more cloud formation, less sunlight, and more wet, cool weather, ideal for colds, pneumonia, and influenza.*

# Air Pollution 'Causes Most Human Diseases'

TORONTO (CP) – Air pollution causes more than half of all human diseases, Dr. Joseph McKenna, of Toronto, yesterday told a public inquiry into pollution.

He said that air pollution plays a role in lung cancer and, by "irrefutable medical evidence," is held responsible for more than 50 per cent of all diseases in man.

Urban areas are hard hit because of weather conditions which cause a buildup of pollutants.

"People with reasonably normal lungs have enough reserves and protection to survive with slight discomfort.

"But those children predisposed to asthma or those older individuals with impaired respiratory mechanism become seriously ill, or even succumb under this added stress."

He said that, as a surgeon, he has become increasingly aware "it is not adequate to just treat the results of pollution with drugs or with lung resections.

"We must instead recognize the cause and eliminate it from our environment."

The combustion of fuels such as oil and coal are mainly responsible for the belching of pollutants into the air, he said.

Dr. McKenna explained the characteristic symptoms of pollution-induced ills are coughing spells, sore throats, a sense of suffocation, shortness of breath and bouts of sinusitis.

When pollutants are inhaled, he said, many visual changes occur in the linings of human air passages.

There is an increased secretion of fluid which becomes thick and obstructs small air passages. Tiny hairs on the cells in the airways are paralyzed, stop cleaning out extraneous material, and the cells are destroyed.

Deaths from the common cold, bronchial asthma, chronic bronchitis, pulmonary emphysemal bronchiectasis, can be correlated with the amount and type of fuel used and the sulphur dioxide level of the air, he said.

# We Can Afford Clean Air

## Edmund K. Faltermayer

An astounding 133 million tons of aerial garbage is now being dumped into the U.S. atmosphere each year. If it could be placed on a giant scale, it would outweigh the country's annual steel production. Table I, based on estimates by the U.S. Public Health Service, shows which human activities are responsible for this rising torrent of contamination, and what each activity's ugly brew consists of. The chart shows only the five pollutants that account for most of the over-all tonnage; not shown are scores of other gases and stinks that defile the nation's air.

These pollutants are eating away at fabrics and metals. They are defacing buildings and spoiling crops. The government estimates the property damage alone at $11 billion a year, and this does not include the decline in real estate values in neighborhoods with air that is second class or worse. Air pollution also represents a prodigious waste of potentially valuable resources: the harmful sulphur dioxide that is

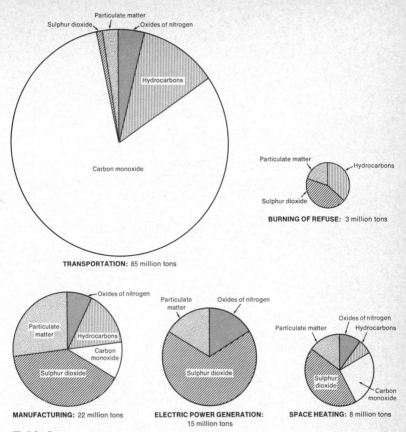

Table I.

vented to the atmosphere each year, for example, contains about $300 million worth of sulphur at today's prices. While medical researchers have not proved that any of these pollutants is injuring large numbers of people, this junk obviously is doing our systems no good. "There is no longer any doubt," Surgeon General Luther L. Terry declared nearly three years ago, "that air pollution is a hazard to health." In agreement, the American Medical Association recently called for "maximum feasible reduction of all forms of air pollution."

Besides damaging health and property and wasting resources, air pollution dejects and degrades the human spirit in ways that a civilized society should not tolerate. The acrid smog associated with automobile exhausts, once confined to Los Angeles but now turning up elsewhere, probably does not kill people. It merely envelops them in an ugly yellow haze that blots out the view and smarts the eyes. The pride of Denver – the prospect of the Rocky Mountains from downtown streets – is often obscured these days by a man-made cloud of pollution. New Yorkers, plagued with 12,000 soot-spewing apartment-house incinerators, literally inhale a portion of their own garbage. In St. Louis, a survey showed, 39 per cent of the people are dogged by noisome odors. After poor schools and inadequate play space, air pollution is probably the most important single factor driving the middle class to the suburbs, and a portion of the country's commuting woes must be ascribed to it. Renascent cities are trying to lure these citizens back, but they recoil from air that is dirty, malodorous, and menacing.

The U.S. has both the technology and the wealth to reduce pollution drastically. Even though thousands of factories are still discharging their wastes into the public air, most of the devices for controlling emissions from industrial plants were invented years ago. "We can handle just about any pollution-control demand that is likely to be made," says John E. Schork, president of Research-Cottrell, Inc., a leading maker of pollution-abating devices. Cleaning up automobile emissions and the sulphur dioxide from electric power stations still presents engineering problems, but solutions will undoubtedly be found in the next few years.

Money is not a problem, either. The nationwide application of the best techniques either already or soon to be available would cost the country far less than is generally believed. An expenditure of less than one-half of 1 percent of the gross national product – probably about $3 billion a year – would reduce air pollution by at least two-thirds. By drastically reducing that $11 billion a year of property damage, the expenditure would easily pay for itself.

With the technical skills and the monetary means at hand, it is incredible that we put up with this needless outrage. With an awakened public, there would be no need to employ subsidies and other economic gimmicks to hasten industry's cleanup, as some experts have proposed. Corporations can absorb many of these expenditures anyway, and consumers would not notice them in the prices of the things they buy. Indeed, households would probably feel the costs of a national rollback of air pollution only in the prices of two items, electricity and new cars. But these two items are so universal that price increases, rather than subsidies, would be a perfectly equitable way to distribute the burden. The role of the federal government, *Fortune* believes, can largely be confined to the setting of standards, and to aiding state and local governments in enforcement.

## What's Done Is Too Little

A good deal is already being done about air pollution, to be sure. Thanks to the Clean Air Act of 1963, which for the first time made matching federal grants available for state and local enforcement efforts, dozens of localities have set up control programs. While many companies have waited until local authorities forced them to clean up, some enlightened managements have designed new factories more tightly controlled than local regulations require. Exact figures are not available, but industry is probably spending about $300 million a year on the installation and operation of special equipment, changes in materials and production processes, and on research designed to abate air pollution. Spending by government at all levels on enforcement and research now is running at $35 million annually, about three-fifths of it federal money. The national effort may grow larger now that Congress has passed a bill by Senator Edmund S. Muskie of Maine that, among other things, enables the Secretary of Health, Education, and Welfare to order the nationwide installation on new cars of devices to limit the pollution from tail pipes.

But all the present efforts, even combined with those under serious consideration, may not permit us to hold our own. During the next forty years the population of the country's urban areas is expected to double, and industrial output and automobile ownership in these same urban zones will grow even faster. The emissions from each factory chimney, automobile tail pipe, and other sources will have to be reduced more than 50 percent on the average, just to keep the urban air from becoming any fouler than it already is. If the air is to be *improved*, the clampdown on emissions will obviously have to be even tighter.

In the case of "stationary" sources of air pollution like factories, incinerators, and electric power stations, the present effort is far too small to bring about any significant advances. The only pollutants of this kind that have been reduced noticeably are the nongaseous, largely nontoxic dusts and fumes that come under the general heading of "particulate matter." Chicago's "dust fall" has declined since the 1930's, and Pittsburgh and St. Louis no longer experience darkness at noon. But this improvement was helped along by the switch from coal for heating, and the switching is nearly complete. As the rainfall of dust and soot on Manhattan's East Side (eighty tons a month per square mile) testifies, particulate matter is still an abominable nuisance in many areas. In fast-industrializing cities like Denver, it is on the increase.

Meanwhile, emissions of the far more dangerous gaseous pollutants are rising dramatically. If recent trends continue, the emission of sulphur dioxide from electric power stations – the largest single source – will increase sixfold by the year 2000. The control devices recently developed for autos, even if adopted across the nation, will bring no lasting rollback in carbon monoxide and hydrocarbon emissions, since these gains will be more than canceled out by rising automobile registrations, which are doubling every twenty-five years.

In the longer-range future, the increase in the airborne wastes thrown off by man's activities may require some drastic solutions. The tremendous rise in the worldwide use of fossil fuels, some authorities say, is putting carbon dioxide into the atmosphere faster than plants and the ocean can absorb it. This gas, which is the unavoidable result of all combustion, is not a "pollutant" in the ordinary sense of being harmful or annoying. But carbon dioxide produces a "greenhouse effect," and tends to block the radiation back to outer space of some of the heat energy that the earth absorbs from the sun. The carbon dioxide concentration in the atmosphere has increased about 8 percent since 1890, and may account for the slight warming up of the Northern Hemisphere

*City Hall, Toronto. These two photographs were taken from the 54th floor of the Toronto-Dominion Centre, facing north. At 8.15 a.m., the time of the view on the left, the city was under a severe temperature*

*inversion. Three hours later, at 11.15, the rising temperature combined with a light breeze to disperse most of the polluted air. The camera positions and settings were the same for both photographs.*

since then. In a study two years ago, the Conservation Foundation found this carbon dioxide buildup "not yet alarming," but said it might eventually cause the polar ice caps to melt, submerging many of the world's cities. To this kind of threat, the only answer might be a large-scale switchover to nuclear power, which produces no carbon dioxide.

### The Dump Has Its Limits

While the carbon dioxide buildup will bear close watching in the years ahead, the immediate task is to cleanse the air of those 133 million tons of dirt and poison that are annually pouring into it. The atmosphere's limitations as a dumping ground for this kind of junk have already become obvious. There are 90 trillion tons of air over the forty-eight contiguous states at any given time. Last year's load of pollutants, if released in an instant and evenly dispersed, would amount to only 1.5 parts per million in the air. Since the contamination actually is spread over a year and continually falls to the ground or is washed out by rains, the average concentration in the nation's total air supply is considerably less than that. But half of this pollution is emitted from less than 1 percent of the U.S. land area, where 50 percent of the population lives. When winds are slack, this far heavier outpouring can build up to thousands of times the national average.

Things can get even worse when there is also a temperature inversion, in which a warm layer of air aloft acts as a lid atop the contaminants in the cooler surface air. This phenomenon was once thought to be peculiar to Los Angeles, where the lid drops to 500 feet or less 40 percent of the time. Actually, it occurs commonly throughout most of the U.S. In New York and Philadelphia, for example, low-level inversions occur 25 percent of the time, and even more often in the fall. The only real difference is that Los Angeles' inversions tend to be lower, and are accompanied by below-average winds. But New York throws off much more non-automotive air pollution. The air above us is not a boundless ocean. Much of the time it is a shallow, stagnant pond, and we are the fish at the bottom.

### In Los Angeles, Compulsion Brings Results

The most rigid emission standards in the U.S. today are applied in the Los Angeles County Air Pollution Control District. Faced with acute smog conditions, Los Angeles authorities have forced the installation of pollution-limiting devices on California automobiles. They have also forced industry to reduce its emissions by nearly 80 percent since the late 1940's; an estimated 5,000 tons of pollutants a day from stationary sources are now being kept out of the sky. What would be the cost of a "Los Angeles treatment" for all manufacturing? We can get some indication by looking at a few of the major air polluters, such as steel and chemical plants and oil refineries.

The orange clouds of dust – mainly iron oxide – pouring out of smokestacks carry the major pollutants that the steel industry generates. Not long ago steel companies in Chicago, with a combined ingot capacity of about 13 million tons a year, agreed to eliminate all dust by 1971 at a reported capital cost of approximately $30 million. This suggests a cost of about $2.50 per ton of capacity. Since steel companies in several other cities are pushing ahead with controls or replacing open hearths with basic oxygen furnaces – all of which have controls – it appears that as much as two-thirds of the country's approximately 150 million tons of steelmaking capacity may be operating with "clean stacks" by the early 1970's. Generously assuming that it might cost as much as $5 per ton of capacity to equip the remaining third, or about $250 million, the

industry would have approximately to double its spending on air-pollution equipment in the years ahead.

The chemical industry, turning out thousands of different products, emits a bewildering variety of gases and exotic odors. Lots of chemical plants, as one industry spokesman concedes, are "quite flavorsome" to human noses, which have a remarkable sensitivity to noisome odors. A lot of the effluent is potentially dangerous, too. The phosphate fertilizer plants in Polk and Hillsborough counties in Florida used to emit large quantities of fluorides that damaged citrus crops and caused the teeth of cattle to drop out. But in the last five years the plants have installed about $22 million worth of equipment and cut emissions by more than half, while increasing production 43 percent. One of them, faced with a shutdown by a court injunction, managed to reduce its daily fluoride emissions from 900 to 300 pounds in only sixty days. The members of the Manufacturing Chemists Association, which embraces most of the industry, have invested a total of $212 million in air-pollution control facilities to date, and expect to spend another $49 million in the next five years. This does not include additional operating costs or research, which together come to $26,600,000 a year. Rough estimates of what it would cost to bring all the country's chemical plants up to the level of the cleanest ones range up to $500 million just for equipment, not counting outlays already planned, but half that amount might do the job.

The cleanest petroleum refineries in the nation are to be found, not surprisingly, in the Los Angeles area. Standard Oil of California's refinery at El Segundo, partly screened by trees, emits little besides innocuous steam to the atmosphere and cannot be smelled more than half a block away. To comply with Los Angeles' strict rules, oilmen say, would probably add between 5 and 10 percent to the cost of a new refinery. While no recent figures are available, a 1961 survey showed that U.S. petroleum refineries were spending about $18 million a year on pollution-abatement equipment. But 44 percent of the money was being spent on the West Coast. Bringing all U.S. refineries up to Los Angeles standards, therefore, might require the expenditure of an additional $10 million a year on equipment. Some of this would pay for itself by recovering valuable substances. Indeed, it has been estimated that four-fifths of the sulphur dioxide which U.S. petroleum refineries might otherwise be venting to the atmosphere is now captured as sulphuric acid or elemental sulphur.

*The Particulars on Particulate Matter*

The troublesome pollutants from electric power stations are particulate matter, in the form of fly ash and sulphur dioxide. The first comes almost entirely from coal-burning generating plants, and the techniques for controlling it have been around for decades. In 1962, according to the Edison Electric Institute, private power companies kept nine million tons of fly ash from entering the sky, far more than the approximately two million tons that escaped. Electrostatic precipitators in the newest plants catch 99 percent of the stuff, and a still newer unit at a mine-mouth plant going up in western Pennsylvania will be the first in the U.S. to remove 99.5 percent. Unfortunately, new plants are still being built in some areas with mechanical collection systems that keep no more than 70 percent out of the air. To bring all the country's 130 million kilowatts of coal-burning generating capacity up to the 99.5 percent level might cost about $300 million.

The cost of collecting fly ash has only a negligible effect on the price of electricity – well under 1 percent by one estimate, counting the write-off of equipment. The control of sulphur dioxide, on the other hand, could have a sizable effect on consumers' monthly bills. Electric generating stations are the country's biggest single source of this gas, and capturing it before it goes out the stack is one of the really tough problems in cleaning up the air. Most of the gas comes from the burning of coal, which contains about 2.5 percent sulphur on the average, and which is used to generate 54 percent of the nation's electricity. Oil accounts for a much smaller share, but heavy residual fuel oil, which generally has about the same percentage of sulphur, is used extensively in places like New York City.

Sulphur dioxide is the most worrisome of the major pollutants, and 23 million tons of it are currently being discharged into the country's air. It has been implicated in most of the famous air-pollution disasters, such as the 1948 one at Donora, Pennsylvania (twenty dead), and the 400 "excess deaths" recorded during a fifteen-day smog episode in New York City early in 1963. While not toxic to man in the concentrations ordinarily found in the atmosphere, it can cause acute crop damage in relatively small concentrations. In industrial regions it causes nickel to corrode twenty-five times as fast as in rural air, and copper five times as fast. And under certain conditions it kills people. One of its derivatives, sulphuric acid mist, can get past the body's natural filtration system and penetrate deep into the lungs, causing severe damage. While the sulphur dioxide in New York City, which has the highest concentration, averages only 0.16 parts per million, it has flared up as high as 2.64 ppm – enough to kill some persons already suffering from respiratory ailments.

Until now, no economically feasible way has been found to curb the emissions of this gas from coal- and oil-burning power stations. The only solution has been for the electric companies to build tall stacks so that the sulphur dioxide will not reach the ground until it is far away and greatly diluted. But electric-power consumption in the U.S. is doubling every twelve years, and the consumption of coal by utilities is expected to rise almost as rapidly in the years ahead. Some air-pollution men already question the efficacy of building ever higher stacks in the nation's fast-spreading metropolitan complexes. Nor will atomic power or natural gas – which contains very little sulphur – be of much help in the years just ahead.

There appear to be only two ways out. In the case of residual fuel oil, local authorities could require power companies to switch to No. 2 oil, which is low in sulphur but costs 80 percent more. Or petroleum companies could take part of the sulphur out of residual oil, raising its price 20 to 30 percent. As for coal, the only answer is to trap the sulphur dioxide after the fuel is burned, and to convert it to marketable acid or elemental sulphur. The Department of Health, Education, and Welfare is planning to spend $7 million to build pilot models of some systems that show promise of being able to make such a conversion economically. Recently, officials of the Bureau of Mines estimated that any one of the three leading processes would impose an added cost, even when allowance was made for the sale of acid or sulphur, equivalent to an increase in fuel costs of 10 to 25 percent. The estimates, it should be noted, are based on the installation of these processes in a new, 800,000-kilowatt plant. The capital expense of fitting them into existing power stations, other studies show, would be much higher, perhaps doubling the augmented cost.

These figures are not quite so gloomy as they look. Fuel represents only about one-seventh of the total cost of generating and distributing electricity, or about 2.5 mills per kilowatt-hour. Even if the power companies were forced to burn low-sulphur fuel or were directed both to install sulphur dioxide recovery systems in new coal stations and to fit out similarly all the existing ones, the cost of the electricity generated by them – about 600 billion kilowatt-hours last year – would probably not rise by more than $600 million a year.

*Traffic in Carbon Monoxide*

In terms of sheer tonnage, the automobile is the country's No. 1 air polluter. According to Public Health Service estimates, it accounts for over four-fifths of the 85 million tons of contaminants emitted by all forms of transportation, including trucks, buses, railroads, and airlines. The three dangerous and obnoxious ingredients issuing from the nation's 72 million automobile tail pipes are carbon monoxide, unburned hydrocarbons, and oxides of nitrogen. While it can kill a man by depriving his blood of its oxygen-carrying capabilities, carbon monoxide is generally not dangerous in open places. Nevertheless, it can reach dangerous concentrations in heavily traveled city intersections and expressways. Biochemist A. J. Haagen-Smit of California Institute of Technology says the level frequently gets to 30 ppm on the Los Angeles freeways – enough to deprive the blood of 5 percent of its oxygen capacity if inhaled for eight hours – and sometimes reaches 120 ppm in traffic jams. More trouble per ton is caused by the unburned hydrocarbons, some of them highly reactive, that spew out of cars. Their partners in crime are the oxides of nitrogen. All forms of combustion, particularly in motor vehicles and electric power stations, give off nitric acid. Most of this is quickly converted into nitrogen dioxide, a whiskey-brown gas that is five times as toxic. When the sun shines on a mixture of hydrocarbons and nitrogen dioxide on a warm day, the result is photochemical smog.

The automobile industry has opposed controls on automobile exhaust emissions outside Los Angeles on the unpersuasive ground that other cities do not yet have an acute smog problem. But Washington, D.C., where the number of cars per square mile is three times as great as in the Los Angeles metropolitan area, has already had some eye-watering days. Denver figures that 40 percent of its pollution comes from the automobile, and in New York City the car contributes a third. "We didn't have that haze until they built the expressways," says a Chicago air-pollution man, "but we sure have it now."

Most of the radical proposals for dealing with smog. even if adopted, would barely enable cities to hold their own. Turbine-powered vehicles, now being tested by the auto manufacturers, are low in pollution ("It would make your eyes bug out, it's that low," enthuses a Chrysler man), but have not yet proved out. Diesel engines are noisier and costlier than the gasoline engine and, while they emit less carbon monoxide and hydrocarbons, they produce just as much oxides of nitrogen.

The only solution, for the foreseeable future, is to clean up the internal-combustion engine. Since 1963 the automobile companies have installed crankcase devices that vent back into the intake manifold the unburned gases that push past piston rings during combustion. But these "blow-by" devices, which actually were used on some makes years ago and then dropped, reduce only one of the car's three pollutants, hydrocarbons, and by only 30 percent. For this reason, California state authorities, who seek to roll back the pollution in Los Angeles to the 1940 level, have insisted on controlling exhaust emissions. Chrysler Corp. has a "cleaner air package," which meets California's standards, and adds $13 to $25 to the price of a new car. The device, which sends a leaner mixture to the engine and advances the spark during deceleration for more complete burning of fuel, can be maintained for only a dollar a year more than the cost of a recommended engine tune-up, Chrysler claims. The other three auto companies have announced systems that, like Chrysler's, alter fuel-air mixture and timing. But they have added a pump that injects air into the exhaust manifold to aid the burn-up of contaminants. This system would increase the price of a new car by as much as $50. These devices are appearing for the first time on 1966-model cars sold in California.

## *Forcing Detroit to "Find Something"*

The combination of crankcase "blow-by" device and exhaust controls, California authorities say, will reduce carbon monoxide emissions by 60 percent and hydrocarbons by about 70 percent. But, it will be ten years before 85 percent of the cars now on the road have them, and meanwhile the number of automobiles in the Los Angeles area may grow faster than smog is reduced. For this reason the state has ordered a further 15 percent cutback by 1970. At the moment, Detroit does not know how it will comply. "We have to find something, don't ask me what," says an official at General Motors' Warren, Michigan, research center. In addition, California may shortly set limits for emissions of oxides of nitrogen. The auto industry does not yet know how to control these, either, since they present totally different problems. But it seems safe to assume that Detroit will come up with something if it has to.

Now that Senator Muskie's bill has been passed, it is fairly certain that the Secretary of Health, Education and Welfare will set automobile emission standards for the entire U.S. While reluctant to do so – even though it makes money on them – Detroit says it can install the control devices on all new cars beginning with 1968 models. In a nine-million car year, this would add as much as $400 million to what the public spends on automobiles. The later adoption of controls on oxides of nitrogen might conceivably double this figure, to about $800 million.

Any increase in the cost of gasoline-powered cars would improve the prospects for electric cars. Yardney Electric Corp. of New York City already has a special Renault Dauphine fitted with lightweight batteries that can propel it at speeds up to fifty-five miles an hour, and up to eighty miles on a charge. The catch is that these are military-type silver-zinc batteries costing $3,000. Nevertheless, several companies, including Yardney and General Dynamics Corp., are pushing ahead in the search for batteries that would cost only a fraction of this. Electric-utility men, of course, yearn for ways to put their off-peak generating capacity to use, and become rhapsodic at the vision of millions of battery-operated cars plugged in nightly for recharging. While a battery-operated car suitable for long journeys is a long way off, a smaller version might be available in a few years.

## Smoldering Trash Fires

Not counting manufacturing wastes, Americans now generate 150 million tons of trash and garbage a year. About half of that mountain of waste is burned. But the conditions under which much of the burning takes place can be fairly primitive. In Denver back-yard incinerators account for 25 percent of the total air pollution. In Chicago many apartment houses still burn their garbage in heating boilers. Under these conditions, noisome odors and tons of soot spill over whole neighborhoods – an affront to the nostrils and a major cleaning problem.

The best prevailing practice is to construct large municipal incinerators. New York City has done this, but its incinerators are not equipped with precipitators, and they discharge into the air eight pounds of particulate matter for every ton of mixed trash and garbage burned. Yet they are immaculate affairs compared to the city's apartment-house incinerators, which spew out twenty-six pounds per ton. "It's like permitting outhouses," says a Los Angeles air-pollution man. But such conditions do not have to be tolerated: Europe's newest municipal incinerators not only are equipped with precipitators, but take advantage of the fuel value of rubbish to make steam and electricity.

It would not cost catastrophic sums for American cities to abate the nuisance caused by the burning of rubbish. New York City will shortly begin requiring double-flue incinerators in new apartment buildings, which will produce relatively little soot. Another solution would be to outlaw the construction of any incinerators in apartment houses, and to require modifications on the 12,000 existing ones. But since this far-from-ideal solution would cost the owners as much as $60 million, it might make more sense to shut the incinerators down and spend about $15 million to build a city incinerator that could reduce the soot and fumes by 99 percent. The city resists this idea because it figures that the added cost of hauling the refuse to an incinerator would be $19 million a year. But if it were hauled, and if precipitators were installed on all existing municipal incinerators, and if all capital equipment were written off over a ten-year period, the total additional cost of doing the job right would work out to a piddling 25 cents a month for each of the city's eight million residents.

## The Burning Question

While small on a per capita basis, such expenditures would be large enough to present real problems in many areas. Between now and 1985, the Public Health Service has estimated, cities and towns may have to spend $506 million on municipal incinerators just to handle the expected increase in refuse collections. If the cost of building incinerators to handle a larger share of the existing load were included, that figure could easily be doubled. And this does not count the added cost of collecting and burning the stuff, which could easily total $2 billion a year. Not all of this represents the cost of abating air pollution, since most of these facilities may have to be built anyway to rid communities of heaps of refuse. But about a third of these operating and capital expenses, or an average of about $350 million a year between now and 1985, could be somewhat arbitrarily assigned to the cost of cleaning up the city air.

In view of the enormous costs of handling refuse, more cities are exploring ways to make some economic use of it. In addition to steam generation, some cities have recently gone over to the practice, long popular in Europe, of composting refuse and selling it to farmers as a soil conditioner. Ross McKinney, director of the University of Kansas' environmental health laboratory, has devised another system that is similar to composting except that it is anaerobic – i.e., the refuse is broken down in the absence of oxygen. This not only cuts the bulk in half and produces a soil conditioner of possible value, but liberates a lot of methane gas, which could be used to generate power. McKinney, who frets that the U.S. is doing only about $500,000 worth of research a year on ways to dispose of rubbish, foresees trash-carrying pipelines in cities that will eliminate costly pickup services.

*Not Free as Air, but . . .*

In sum, cleaning up our badly soiled atmosphere is well within this country's means. To apply the best existing abatement techniques to all the plants in three main branches of manufacturing, not counting expenditures already under way, and effectively to curb fly-ash emissions throughout the country's present electric generating facilities, would require an expenditure on equipment of about $1 billion. This figure allows for the fact that it usually costs 25 to 30 percent more to install emission-curbing devices in an old plant than to design them into new ones. It should be doubled to take in all other branches of industry, and redoubled to include operating costs. Thus the cost of bringing the country's present industrial establishment up to the current level of technical knowledge in the field, if spaced over ten years, would run about $400 million a year. Meanwhile, industry could easily double what it is spending to curb air pollution in its *new* facilities – presumably where most of its current $300 million of spending is directed. Altogether, the application of the best existing technology to industry would cost about $1 billion a year.

This is a liberal estimate. Industry in Los Angeles County, where the strictest regulations prevail, has been spending about $2.30 a year for each of the area's residents, which would work out to a figure of about $450 million for the nation. This probably understates things, however, as Los Angeles does not have as much heavy industry of the air-polluting type as some other areas. But despite this qualification, it is evident that U.S. industry could achieve standards of cleanliness like those of Los Angeles for far less than the $50-billion to $75-billion estimate given last year by a corporate witness at a Senate hearing.

To this $1 billion a year must be added the $600 million it might cost to remove sulphur dioxide from the flue gases of the utilities, the $800 million it could cost to apply all the foreseeable controls to the automobile, and the $350 million cost of ensuring soot-free rubbish disposal. These would boost the price of cleaner air to about $2.75 billion a year. Even if a few other items are tossed in – such as a ban on the use of high-sulphur fuel for home heating, programs to reduce the oxides of nitrogen emitted by electric utilities and to deodorize diesel exhausts, more research, and a fivefold step-up in state and local enforcement activities – it is difficult to see how the total could greatly exceed $3 billion a year. And this estimate makes almost no allowance for offsetting savings to industry from the recovery of marketable products. Also, it assumes there will be no major cost-cutting break-throughs in controlling sulphur dioxide or in cleaning up automobile exhaust – an assumption that could turn out to be unduly pessimistic. This program will not buy city air as pure as that which greeted the Pilgrim Fathers at Plymouth Rock. But it would reduce total pollution by at least two-thirds, so that we would only occasionally be aware of it.

For $1.30 a month each, we could all breathe easier.

*Keeping out the Feds*

Unfortunately, American industry does not have a record it can be proud of in the abatement of pollution. Many corporations are reluctant to clean up voluntarily so long as their competitors in areas with weak or nonexistent air-pollution enforcement are going scot free. And the idea of a uniform clampdown across the nation is anathema to most industrial spokesmen. Conditions vary from place to place, they argue. New York's air is high in dust and sulphur dioxide but low in automotive smog, while Los Angeles' situation was the opposite. Therefore, they say, it is wasteful to crack down uniformly on all pollutants in all cities. In rebuttal, however, some experts point out that it made sense for Los Angeles, which had lower sulphur dioxide readings than most cities, to curb emissions of this damaging gas as well.

Impatient with industry's progress, some economists have been exploring ways to speed it up. A special committee under Gardner Ackley, chairman of the Council of Economic Advisers, has been considering the feasibility of imposing a scale of charges on companies that pollute the air. Tax concessions in the form of faster write-offs, and a doubling of investment credits when equipment for controlling pollution is installed, have also been suggested. But a system of charges would be incredibly complicated to administer because of the difficulty of identifying and metering aerial contamination. Tax concessions, which in effect are subsidies, are objectionable because they amount to bribing companies to be good citizens; the federal government might as well arrange a payment to every child who refrains from dropping candy wrappers in the street. The experience of Los Angeles, where no economic gimmicks were employed, shows what can be accomplished by local enforcement.

Washington's role, in fact, can be a limited one. It seems clear, from industry's dismal record, that national standards for emission are needed for every industrial process. The federal government is best equipped to carry on the research needed to establish these standards.

Their actual enforcement, however, can best be done by state and local governments. The federal government has limited policing powers under the 1963 law, and can intervene in interstate air-pollution situations if localities move too slowly (about 40 million people live in urban zones that straddle state lines), or in an intrastate situation if the governor requests it. But the main federal contribution to enforcement should be money. In the past year, when matching grants from Washington have become available for the first time, they have brought a 47 percent increase in the budgets of state and local air-pollution control agencies. Federal money spent in this way is far more potent than direct subsidies would be, and much less of it will be needed.

# Part B

# Water:
# What Went Wrong?

92 *Man the Modifier*

| | |
|---|---|
| Sophisticated Oil Pollution Detectors Coming | 124 |
| Mercury Spills in More Rivers | 126 |
| Dow Won't Compensate Fishermen | 127 |
| Polluters Are Thieves: Kerr | 129 |
| Private Phosphate Probe Follows Gov't 'Secret' | 130 |
| 10% of Cottages Pollute Lakes: Task Force | 132 |
| Why Lakes Become Green and Slimy | 135 |

*Barely 2% of the world's water is fresh, and Man is working hard at reducing this to zero. Chemicals, phosphates, road salt, nitrates, industrial acids, pesticides, commercial and municipal wastes combine to make pure water more difficult to find, and fresh water more expensive to purify. The question arises of whether the water user should be charged with cleaning it.*

*In* The Shame of Our Ottawa River *the writer points out that "Quebec has without a doubt the worst pollution control record of any Province." This is amply reflected in the statistic that the Quebec Water Board receives $700,000 dollars per year, while the Ontario Water Resources Commission receives $42 million.*

# The Shame of Our Ottawa River

**Wade Rowland**

> *"The resulting pollution is not difficult to imagine. At the Rideau locks sewer outfall, tourists taking the sightseeing tour down the Ottawa River on pleasure boats first have to pass through a patch of water where floating faeces, toilet tissue, oil, soapy water and other debris can be seen . . ."*
>
> From an Ontario Water Resources Commission report on pollution of the Ottawa River.

OTTAWA – You don't have to be an expert to tell the Ottawa River is polluted. On a hot day, you can smell it from inside the House of Commons.

The Quebec Water Board has described the stretch of the river from the Rideau rapids near Ottawa to Lake of Two Mountains 50 miles downstream as "nothing but a vast bubbling swamp."

In a 1965 report the Quebec agency stated that over the same 50 miles of river the dissolved oxygen content of the water has been so dramatically lowered by pollution that most fish would suffocate in it. The picture has not changed.

One of the principal reasons why the Ottawa remains an open sewer has been the apparent lack of interest on the part of the Quebec Provincial government in the subject of water pollution.

Quebec has, without a doubt, the worst pollution control record of any province.

While Ontario has reached the point where every community on the south shore of the river has either installed a sewage treatment plant or has one under way, there is not one municipal treatment facility anywhere on the Quebec side of the shared waterway.

Of the 144,000 Quebeckers who live along the north shore of the Ottawa, more than 90 percent dump their raw sewage directly into the river.

In downtown Hull, a Canada Packers plant discharges animal wastes of every description in enormous quantities into Brewery Creek, which flows into the Ottawa well within the national capital area.

The Quebec Water Board estimates the packing plant waste amounts to the equivalent of raw sewage from a city of 130,000 inhabitants.

It is extremely high in dangerous bacteria, and is so blatantly offensive it is advisable not to look at it on a full stomach.

Canada Packers has made Brewery Creek, actually a deep, fast-flowing river, the most disgustingly polluted stretch of water to be found in Canada.

Despite this, it is apparent that the company has never been asked by the Quebec government to clean up its effluent.

The city of Hull, far from seeking action on its own, uses the same waterway as a garbage dump, in violation of several Federal statutes.

It is an astounding sight to see tractors ploughing household trash into what once was a particularly scenic waterway, almost within sight

of Parliament Hill where the laws prohibiting such action were so solemnly debated.

But all other industrial and municipal polluters of the Ottawa River pale when compared to the pulp and paper industry.

The waste from the eight paper mills spotted along the length of the river is approximately equivalent to the raw sewage from the combined populations of the cities of Toronto, Montreal and Ottawa.

Of the eight – Canadian International Paper Co. in Temiscaming, Hawkesbury and Gatineau, Consolidated Bathurst at Portage du Fort, E. B. Eddy Co. in Ottawa and Hull, James MacLaren at Masson and Thurso Paper at Thurso – only Consolidated Bathurst has to date made a concerted effort to improve the quality of its effluent, according to Ontario Water Resources Commission and Quebec Water Board sources.

The mills on the Ontario side have come under withering fire in recent months from the Ontario Water Resources Commission, which has demanded a speedy clean-up, imposing a stringent timetable.

*Merry Way*

But in Quebec, the industry has been allowed to go its merry way, secure in the knowledge that the Quebec Water Board has been instructed by government not to make public statistics on the staggering damage being done to the river's life-system.

By contrast, most of the huge mass of data compiled over the years by the OWRC is public information, and is in fact used effectively by the commission to build public backing for its industrial and municipal clean-up programs.

But the most telling comparison of the attitudes of the two provincial governments to the water pollution crisis lies in the fact that the Quebec Water Board is allotted a meagre $700,000 a year from public funds. The OWRC's budget is $42 million.

One four-year-old Quebec Water Board report which the province saw fit not to release points out that:

"At Gatineau (location of one of Canadian International Paper's plants) and for a considerable distance downstream, aquatic animal life has been *eliminated* and the river bed is covered with a thick layer of decomposing fibres.

"This is the most repulsively ugly stretch of the Ottawa River."

Tests done by the OWRC on the Ontario side of the Ottawa have shown that the situation is comparable wherever a pulp mill dumps its effluent into the river.

*Explosive*

The pulp waste lining the river bed is so thoroughly impregnated with chemicals that samples collected by commission technicians must be stored in formaldehyde to prevent sample jars from exploding when exposed to room temperature air.

Commission scientists feel that predictions that this waste would be flushed from the river within about 10 years of a complete halt to dumping are extremely optimistic.

Pulp mill effluent is deadly to fish in several ways.

Near the mouth of sewer lines, toxic chemicals are found in high enough concentrations to poison all animal life.

However, in a river the size of the Ottawa, these chemicals are quickly diluted and broken down into less deadly materials. The problem is that large amounts of the river's oxygen content is used in the chemical break-down process, and this leaves less oxygen to support fish and other aquatic life.

*Waste discharge from pulp mill, Hull, Quebec.*

Wood fibres discharged by the ton by most mills are also deadly to fish.

They collect in the animals' gills, causing eventual death by suffocation.

The fibre waste also destroys spawning grounds when it settles to the river bed.

Those fish that manage to survive in the area of a pulp mill are made unfit for human consumption by a chemical reaction still little understood by scientists which leaves the fish tasting of kerosene.

Effluent from pulp mills also affects fish life by destroying the smaller animals fish feed on.

Each time a power dam is thrown across a river, its rate of flow is reduced. As the flow drops, so does the river's ability to rejuvenate itself after absorbing oxygen-demanding pollution. On the Ottawa, this reduction of capacity has been significant.

The Quebec Water Board noted this in reporting on the Carillon dam's relation to the pollution problem:

"The dam . . . has considerably reduced the oxygenation rate of the Ottawa River, imposing on municipalities and industries high demands for efficient treatment if reasonable oxygen levels are to be re-established."

These "high demands," needless to say, are not being met by Quebec industries and municipalities. They are, in fact, being completely ignored.

In any other setting, the city of Ottawa would likely come in for severe criticism for failing to give its sewage anything but primary treatment. It is, after all, the nation's showplace.

*By Great Lakes standards, Lake Erie is shallow. Consequently, the
natural aging process proceeds more rapidly there than in the other
lakes. This fact, combined with the millions of gallons of raw sewage and
other wastes poured in from Detroit and other large cities along the
shoreline, has caused Lake Erie to become almost "dead".*

*Among the first to suffer seriously from this were the Erie fishermen.*

# An Eerie Silence
# Settles Over Erie

## John Flanders

Last Tuesday 28-year-old Robert Foot stepped from his tug to a Port
Burwell wharf and listened stunned as a village youth said fishing had
been banned on Lake Erie.

Sceptical, Foot approached local fisherman, processor and retailer
Frank Williams. "What kind of horsefeathers is this," he asked.

"It's not horsefeathers," was the reply. "We've had it."

Probably the most dramatic message in the history of commercial
fishing on the north shore of Lake Erie will arrive Monday from a
federal fisheries department laboratory in Winnipeg.

The very livelihood of Erie fishermen now depends on a 200-pound
sample of Lake Erie perch under analysis.

If the fish, taken from central and eastern basin ports such as Stanley,
Dover and Rowan, show the serious mercury contamination that ended
fishing in Lake St. Clair last week, fishing could be finished.

There's no question about it – fishermen are worried sick.

Since Tuesday's federal order that banned the sale and export of all
perch and pickerel caught commercially, fishermen from Port Maitland
to Erieau have gathered in tense groups in dockside fishing huts.

The situation remains in flux so countless telephone calls to Ottawa
have produced nothing concrete.

J. Henry Misner, secretary-treasurer of the Port Dover fishing and
processing firm, Henry H. Misner Ltd., said government officials told
him yesterday they think the matter should be cleared up by Monday.

*Publicity*

Meanwhile a gale that had kicked around Lake Erie for 24 hours continued to blow and only smelt trawlers were working yesterday.

And even if perch fishermen could move out, their catches would join
thousands of pounds of fish under seizure in packing houses at Kings-
ville, Wheatley, Erieau and Port Stanley.

Fishermen, bitter about the whole deal, say it may take years for the perch market to recover, whether mercury contamination is proven or not – simply because of the publicity.

"Sick to your stomach. That's how it felt," said Foot's father, George, 60, a fisherman since he was eight years old. "I had bologna for dinner today."

George Foot's Wednesday catch of 600 pounds, worth $138 at 23 cents a pound, was seized immediately.

Orville Liberty, 37, of Port Burwell, expects to be paid sometime for 200 pounds he caught before the blow. He doesn't know what to expect for 300 pounds he caught Tuesday and an additional 600 the following day that were seized.

Eight years ago Mr. Liberty lost a lung to cancer and now he captains one of 13 tugs that fish out of Burwell. If perch fishing is banned, he and about 30 other Burwell men will be looking for work, and for those over 50 years of age, it won't be easy.

"We can't change our crops out there like a farmer. The tugs can't be changed over for something else," said fisherman Larry Martin.

"There's nothing else we can do with them. The scrap value is nil. Our trade is peculiar to itself. We're beat."

Today fishermen can't even give fresh perch away, and they place the blame squarely in the laps of federal officials who, they claim, made irresponsible statements to the press before sufficient investigation had been conducted.

And they accuse the press of "crucifying" fishermen by blowing controversy all out of proportion. One fisherman said he hopes to see equally bold headlines if the perch are declared free of mercury.

George Foot said government biologists should have been thoroughly convinced either way about possibilities of contamination before any public statement was made. Second, fishermen should have been notified first.

"They treat us like a bunch of children. The contamination hasn't been proven yet. If those fish come back negative, our processors will say we'll have to freeze the fish for a year until the market gets back on its feet," he said.

"The public is still scared of them and they won't buy."

*Ill-timed*

"This decision was as far as we're concerned taken prior to any conclusive tests being taken or any consultation with the industry," Mr. Misner said. "It is simply a lack of communication."

The decision is ill-timed as well. This time of year is considered the peak time for perch or pickerel because of the spawning and schooling of both species.

Ironically, the controversy comes also when fishermen expected one of their best years of fishing. In 1958, a year after yellow and blue pickerel disappeared from the lake, perch got five cents a pound. In 1959, fishermen were lucky to get three cents. But in the last two years, the perch market has received a couple of boosts – high catches of good quality fish, a government-established floor price of 10 cents a pound and a relatively good market because of high beef prices.

Unlike past years, there were few, if any, perch in storage and a continuing strong demand could have resulted in a substantial increase in the price paid to fishermen.

Lake Erie fishermen harvested a record catch of nearly 30-million pounds valued at $3.2-million in 1969 and this year the federal government earmarked $1-million for a price stabilization program for Erie perch.

On their last paycheque, fishermen got 23 cents a pound for perch, yet fillets cost from 85 cents to $1.05 for the consumer even in Port Burwell.

The infighting between the federal government, responsible for fisheries, and the provincial government, which licences tugs, annoys fishermen too.

Robert Foot said the federal government controls exports, yet if fishermen attempt to negotiate with Ottawa, they are referred to the province. The province, he says, in turn refers him to Ottawa because 90 per cent of the perch catch is exported to the U.S.

"As far as the provincial government is concerned, we're just a nuisance," he said. "There's got to be heads roll. We want to know why and who's responsible.

"There ain't a man who works on the tugs that's afraid of the lake and she's harder on us than any government official. They're attempting to destroy a whole industry."

Although the smelt catch shot up to 16-million pounds last year, the supply is insufficient to support the 160 commercial Erie vessels. The government says smelts are not affected by the mercury.

## Impact

Should fishing be banned, the 160 boats grounded and the 1,000 or so persons who work in processing plants tossed out of a job, the impact on Ontario's economy would be powerful.

Louis Kolbe, president of the Port Dover Fish Co. Ltd., estimates the fishing investment in the town at $2 million. Last year the company's sales amounted to $450,000.

The Misner firm employs about 60 persons in its processing plant and on its six tugs, and the Port Dover Co. plant about 40 persons, although about 250 townspeople work in fishing. In 1969, Misners paid out about $700,000 in wages.

Omstead Fisheries Ltd., in Wheatley, the largest fresh water fisheries in the world, employs an average of 650 persons and Mr. Misner estimates Omstead's 1969 payroll at about $2.5 million.

Port Burwell fishermen believe the impact on the village of about 700, even now in a low income area, would be tragic. "The government would have to subsidize us to bring us up to the poverty level," one fisherman remarked wryly.

Fishing itself doesn't exactly pay a substandard wage, but fishermen feel the province has turned its back on them and they're being used by packing firms which determine prices and control the market. Their concern now is for their women and children.

With most of their perch seized and the uncertainty that they will never be paid, fishermen are discovering employees are failing to show up for work. George Foot must pay his five-man crew in 12 days but hasn't got the money.

"I don't know what the hell I'm going to do for my eight kids," he said. His boat grossed $42,000 last year.

Mr. Liberty, who earned a net of only $6,000 last year has six children. He said that for years he strove to place himself in a secure position in fishing but "now this happens."

## Coverage

He figures it costs about $50 a day just to drive his tug into the lake and return – straight overhead, excluding wages.

Mr. Martin estimates it costs him $15 to $20.

Fishermen say only one man in 20 can take the jostling of a tug and it requires a year of training to make a workhand proficient in handling nets. And then some only earn about $3,000 a year and must work in tobacco during summer when fishing slackens off.

If a ban is imposed, the question of compensation arises. Port Burwell fishermen smoldered with anger when a local MP suggested they sue Dow Chemical in Sarnia, whom the Ontario Water Resources Commission says is the source of the mercury.

"He's got rocks in his head," Mr. Foot said. "We can sue Dow but

*Chemical manufacturing plant, Lake Erie.*

what can we do to feed our bellies while Dow takes it through the courts for five years?"

Some fishermen have already suggested that the federal government would either have to subsidize fishing or buy the tugs out.

But most are optimistic that the 200 pounds of fish in Winnipeg will be found "clean." "It's a heavy metal and it's hard to believe it would get down here," Mr. Kolbe said.

"I don't think there's anyone prepared to take the responsibility of closing down an industry," Mr. Misner said. "How you're going to compensate them I don't know. They wouldn't do it to the extent that would be necessary."

No fisherman has seriously considered alternative jobs, but how can men 50 or 60 years old expect to be hired elsewhere, they ask.

Robert Foot, father of three, said that if necessary he will work in tobacco or become a casual laborer, but emphasized that as soon as any ban is lifted he will return to fishing.

"I'm just stuck. I've got no education," Mr. Liberty said. "I can't get another job too well."

Through the clouds of pessimism, fishermen see at least two benefits of the current controversy. The momentary slowdown in catches will allow perch to spawn and consequently replenish populations.

Secondly, they feel the fisherman's plight has been boldly brought to the attention of the consumer and government.

### Protein

Robert Foot emphasized that fishermen will accept figures of mercury levels – no matter what they turn out to be. But no one has said they are now harmful unless fish are eaten by the ton, and no fisherman expects consumers to eat perch by the ton, he said.

"Fish is a very high protein food. For the average consumer it's a good meal. It's not our fault that the price is so high because we don't see any of that," he said.

"If the fish aren't fit for human consumption, we've got to accept this. Nobody has proved they're poisoned though. If the fish are contaminated, the ban is a good thing. We don't want to poison anybody."

Lake Erie fishermen used to laugh, drink, swear together. Now like their docked tugs, they cluster silently.

"We're in fishing big because we like it, not because we're making money," Robert Foot said. "Fishing is what we want to do. We don't want to work in your steel plants."

# There's Fishing in the Thames Again

LONDON (CP) – Not so long ago the miasma off the Thames was so powerful Parliament had to shut up shop occasionally. The smell became unbearable even through disinfectant-soaked curtains.

When Arthur F. Green went to work on Thames pollution 41 years ago, he says, hardened denizens of Woolwich on the south bank used to be sick in the streets on the river's bad days.

The beautiful bright ships of the P and O line would levy big bills regularly against the London river authorities. The rising whiffs of hydrogen sulphide – the familiar stink-bomb gas of youngsters – quickly darkened their white-leaded hulls to a dirty grey.

And on all the thousands of ships using the bustling river deckhands went crazy as brasswork reverted to a sickly blue almost as soon as it was polished.

"The change has been dramatic," Green says of the way Father Thames, once one of the world's dirtiest rivers, is making an expensive comeback to become one of the cleanest streams in Britain.

Even the fish, which gave up on the Thames a century or so ago, are coming back in numbers. Mostly they are coarse fish, which put up with polluted water the best.

The Thames was a salmon river in the days of Izaak Walton but the salmon fled more than a century ago from the uncontrolled outpouring of raw sewage. Even the coarse fish eventually followed.

Experts agree there is not much chance of the salmon making a comeback after all these years. However, some trout have been turning up in the higher tidal reaches of the river and anglers are hopeful of good fishing later.

It has been a long fight to reverse history in the Thames, which accepted untreated sewage from millions of people for centuries before officials like Green started working on it a couple of generations ago.

Green now is the recognized expert on Thames cleanup. He was scientific adviser to the Greater London Council and on his retirement last year was snapped up by a commercial firm that consults on pollution reduction with the Port of London Authority, which has control over what can be dumped into the 90 miles of tidal Thames.

This control is rigid now. Until recent years it was fairly haphazard and 600,000,000 gallons of sewage – including industrial – a day flowed into the river without much control.

The sewage volume at times is more than the amount of fresh water coming down from above Teddington Lock, the point where the tide stops. However, the wash of the salt water helps keep the pollution level down.

Much of the problem in earlier years came from the fact that the Port of London Authority, while having nominal control of pollution, hadn't much elbow room. For many years it could say only yes or no to a body wanting to discharge into the Thames, without laying down conditions if it said yes. It was reluctant to tell municipal authorities, traditionally putting their sewage into the river, to take it elsewhere if they refused to process it.

The PLA did not get parliamentary authority to impose its own conditions until 1964, though well before that some of the riverside municipalities had gone into sewage treatment on their own.

And just about in time. Some of the Thames's tributaries, including the nobly named Duke of Northumberland's River, were composed mainly of sewage before anti-pollution measures took hold. Now they are clean enough generally for good fishing and for drinking water.

But the pollution fighters have had their troubles.

One municipality that had been sending huge quantities of sewage into Thames tributaries at 22 points built a single treatment plant for all its effluent in the 1930s. One and all assumed its discharge was being cleaned up. It was not until 1963 that some scientific detective work uncovered the fact the plant had gone haywire about 1950 and the municipality had been quietly dumping partly processed "activated sludge" into the big river for 13 years.

Right now, Green says, practically all of the sewage going into the Thames is fully treated – except for that of some riverside industrial plants on which the authorities are putting pressure.

The result is that the oxygen content of the water – which makes the difference between a live stream and a dead one – rises to between 40 and 70 per cent of saturation in some stretches. In a pure stream it would be 95 per cent. Carp, about the toughest of fish, can survive in 25 per cent. In the bad old days, the Thames ran around one per cent.

Cleaning up the Thames has been costing around $60,000,000 a year in treatment plants and other expenses in recent years. From about the filthiest, it has become an example for all of the hundreds of polluted streams in Britain – a problem which is beginning to give the government as much concern as in Canada. A rough estimate of getting them all into shape is $1,000,000,000.

Those delighted fans of the Thames who have been watching its comeback think it worth while.

An appeal for a more widespread program was made in the House of Lords recently by the Earl of Bessborough, whose father was the 1931–35 governor-general of Canada and a noted anti-pollutionist as president of the Royal Sanitary Institute. He said the balance of nature is being upset by lack of fish and insect life in turgid rivers.

In the Thames itself, where no fish life had been known for many generations, there now can be found about 60 varieties – practically all coarse fish at the moment.

There was a graphic illustration of its improvement in the last couple of years. In November, 1968, the Thames Angling and Preservation Society rounded up 36 rod-and-line men for a day on the river. They caught nothing.

Last September in a similar experiment they caught 161 fish, all coarse but big enough for the creel.

And just this winter the first tender-fleshed seafish known to have turned up in the Thames in living memory appeared at Purfleet – 40 miles up-river from the sea. Docker Bernard Hodgetts picked up three haddock stranded by the receding tide as they chased a school of sprat and pronounced them good eating.

"Even at my age," said 66-year-old Arthur Green, "I expect to see the Thames a good fishing river again."

*Some forms of pollution can be controlled by legislation, without placing unreasonable restrictions on the industries concerned. Controls on phosphate detergents, automobile emissions, and oil tanker routes are examples of this kind of approach.*
    Ten-year Pollution Cleanup May Cost $5,000 Million *shows what is being done in Canada, and what the costs are.*

# Ten-year Pollution Cleanup May Cost $5,000 Million

## Basil Jackson

The fight to save the Canadian environment will be long, arduous and costly.

Before the end of this decade, Canadians will have spent an estimated $5,000 million to clean up the mess industrialization, urbanization and increasing population have brought.

For the first time, strong motives and incentives to clean up our environment are present in government, industry and among private citizens. But even to maintain the gains made so far will call for a determined struggle. Making new gains will be a tougher job still.

In some industries – pulp and paper, petroleum, steelmaking – it will take up to eight years before the pollution controls now on the drawing board are installed and fully operative.

But the controls are coming. In British Columbia, Quebec, Ontario and, to a lesser degree, Alberta, Manitoba and Saskatchewan, provincial governments have ordered industries to begin cleaning up.

But in many cases, years will elapse before those orders can be translated into installed equipment and any widespread difference is noticed in the environment.

Even when these controls take effect, it will be unrealistic to expect to see the Great Lakes, for instance, restored to the state of purity they were in when the white man came.

As long as we cling to our present way of life – to our cars, our boats, our industries, in whatever modified form – we are bound to pollute our environment to some extent.

The degree to which we manage to keep it pure – or at least in better condition than it has been – depends on how much we're willing to pay.

Either way, the problem will be costly: either in anti-pollution measures or in despoiled air, soil and water.

What progress have Canadians made toward a solution to the pollution problem since FP reported: "The campaign to eliminate pollution of the air, water and human life is barely started" (June 28, 1969)?

Perhaps the most encouraging trend is the growing awareness that pollution is a global problem.

In a recent reference to the world's first conference on pollution, which the United Nations is sponsoring in Stockholm in 1972, UN Secretary-General U Thant stressed the need for "planetary management" of pollution.

Pollution is an interrelated world problem. For example:
– The approximately 300 four-engined jetliners that daily cross the Atlantic, flying in relatively narrow air lanes, pollute the upper atmosphere with tons of particulates and gases.
– Some British industrialists, in an effort to disperse the smoke from their factory chimneys, built higher stacks. Now Swedes are complaining that the "dirty British smoke" is falling in their country.
– The world's monitoring of radioactive fallout has increased since the French and Chinese tested nuclear bombs, the French in the Pacific and the Chinese on the Asian mainland.

In the past year or two, both Ottawa and the provincial governments have enacted legislation, or improved existing laws, to tighten up pollution controls.

For its part, Ottawa has:
– Passed a law making it illegal to make or import laundry detergents containing more than 20% by weight of phosphates. (Some detergents have as much as 50% phosphates.)

Laundry water containing phosphates, dumped into sewers and from there into rivers and lakes, speeds the growth of algae which, in turn, absorb excessive amounts of oxygen, killing fish and plant life.

So far, detergents for dishwashers have escaped the Ottawa ruling. Dishwasher makers say automatic machines will not work effectively without phosphate-type detergents.

Until stocks of the old laundry detergents are used up, it is impossible to see any improvement being made in lake waters.

– Passed Bill C-137, the Motor Vehicle Safety Act, which includes a phrase – "impairment to health" (see separate article) – that, in effect, gives Ottawa power to control motor-vehicle exhaust pollution across Canada. The bill covers domestically made and imported vehicles.

– Passed Bill C-202, which reduces the risk of pollution of Arctic waters and territory by oil tankers and other ships. The bill specifies structural requirements for ships sailing in Arctic waters, extends Canadian control to 100 miles offshore, and specifies safety control lanes for ships to sail in.

– Passed Bill C-144, the Canada Water Act, under which, with the provinces, the federal government can designate any body of water as a "water quality area" and punish people – up to a $5,000 fine for each offense – for polluting these waters.

The new law also enables Ottawa to implement water-pollution programs of its own on waters that do not come under provincial control.

– Placed an outright ban on the use of an insecticide known as DDD, beginning Jan. 1, 1971. Ottawa placed restrictions on the use of the more familiar DDT last January, which cut its use by about 90%. In May, the government restricted use of weed killer 2,4,5-T. Both DDD and DDT now are classified as health hazards.

Several provinces have tightened their pollution-control legislation in the past year.

The British Columbia Pollution Control Act, for example, was recently amended to make all new industrial sources of air pollutants obtain a permit by Jan. 1, 1971. All existing air-polluting sources are to be registered with the director of the pollution control branch before Dec. 31, 1971.

Armed with these rulings, the B.C. government will have a register of all industrial chimneys and smokestacks, and be able to control their output.

Similar legislation recently was passed to control waste discharges – from new and existing sources – into water and onto soil.

In Ontario, the fines for polluting water are to be increased from $1,000 to $5,000 for each offense. The limits on motor-vehicle exhaust pollution are being made more stringent.

Quebec has no air-pollution control act, largely because municipalities have jurisdiction in the areas where most pollution is created.

Most of the province's dirt-making industries are located in the

Montreal area. In January, 28 municipalities within this area formed the Montreal Urban Community (MUC), with one overall jurisdiction for combatting air pollution.

This long-overdue step now will enable Canada's biggest city to do something about the problem. And already the MUC has passed several stern laws intended to control industrial and residential air pollution.

Some of the new laws, though well-intentioned, are unrealistic.

One, for example, makes it an offense to run the motor of a parked motor vehicle for longer than four minutes. But Montreal will never have enough policemen available to catch out drivers who idle their car engines longer than four minutes before setting out for work on cold winter mornings.

The Quebec Water Board – the equivalent of the Ontario Water Resources Commission – has surveyed the sources of water pollution in the province. It has scheduled a cleanup program that will take 15 years to complete and cost $600 million, including $280 million for full primary and secondary sanitary treatment of raw sewage Montreal now discharges into the St. Lawrence River.

In Ontario, the water resources commission has toughened its attitude toward industrial polluters – pulp and paper, steel and oil-refining companies – and has registered convictions against several firms. The commission has also issued several ministerial orders compelling other offending companies to clean up.

In the past year, media publicity given to pollution has made industry in general extremely sensitive to the problem.

Newspaper and magazine articles, scenes of polluted waterways shown on TV have made many big corporations newly conscious of their responsibilities (although others have long been aware of these responsibilities and have spent millions on cleaning up plant effluent).

But governments have had to prod others into making plans for installing pollution-control equipment.

Exposure of the public to news on pollution has stimulated the formation of citizen groups against pollution across Canada.

Recently, these groups formed a national organization, the Canadian Association of Human Environment, to enable them to bring greater pressure to bear against polluting industries and against governments that do not act to clean up pollution.

The formation of such groups and national organization are symptomatic of a change in the public mood toward pollution. People now are becoming more actively involved in pollution control – forming action groups, writing to government authorities, policing their own habits.

A nationwide demonstration of this concern and involvement will be held Oct. 14, 1970, designated Survival Day.

This is the day, it is hoped by demonstration organizers, on which attention of all Canadians will be focused on the dangers of an ecological disaster – from an accident at a nuclear-power plant, escape of biological-warfare chemicals during disposal – and on mercury contamination of water courses and other sources of air and water pollution.

# New Law Won't Halt Pollution—Prober

A Pollution Prober charged yesterday that the Federal Government's new water pollution legislation allowed polluters to "pay off" and continue to ruin the environment.

Brian Kelly, a member of the grass roots organization undertaken by University of Toronto professors, students and concerned citizens, asked a Federal official:

"How can you put a dollar value on a river? If an ecosystem is destroyed, how can you buy it back with $10,000?"

He and other participants attending a Great Lakes conference at the Education Centre had just heard Dr. A. T. Prince, of the Department of Mines, Energy and Resources, explain the intents and purposes of the New Canada Water Act.

Dr. Prince, an expert in water resources, said industries and municipalities and other sources of waterways pollution would be charged fees for the right to pollute.

He said, too, that pollution would not be defined by the Act, but would be determined instead by regional water quality management boards. These boards would determine how much pollution was acceptable in any of their areas of reference.

His evaluation of the Act, which has yet to come before Parliament, caused shock and disappointment among many at the conference.

Mr. Kelly said he had anticipated that Ottawa planned tough, no-nonsense and no-deal legislation to fight the problem. But as Dr. Prince explained it, polluters will be able to continue polluting by paying fees to the regional water board "commensurate with the degree of pollution."

The regional boards – whose composition has not been determined – would decide how much the levy would be and how it would be used.

He anticipated that the money would be used by the boards to fight the pollution caused by the feepayer. He suggested the fees would be high enough to make the polluter look to installing his own controls.

The regional boards would also have the right to prosecute offenders – and would have the right to do so with degrees of discrimination. They could not, however, force offenders to install pollution control equipment or get out of business.

What this means, Dr. Prince admitted, is that one regional board, going on its self-established definition of pollution, could force a firm into major expense or even out of business, while a similar firm could pollute with impunity in another region.

Mr. Kelly attacked the requirements for control as unequal and asked: "Should anyone have the right to pollute anything?"

Dr. Prince said they did, if they wanted to pay.

# 'Philosophy Change' Needed in Great Lakes Water Use

BUFFALO – Effective water pollution control in the Great Lakes not only needs new political and regulatory institutions, it needs a new approach in philosophy about the use of water.

The problem will never be solved with the present approaches, a New York State University professor said yesterday.

Robert D. Hennigan, director of the State University Water Resources Centre at Syracuse, was speaking yesterday at the 13th Conference on Great Lakes Research.

One traditional approach, what he called the economic-exploitive ethic, was to use natural resources to produce profits, without regard to the environmental consequences.

"The havoc wrought by the runaway economic-exploitive ethic is now being countered by the preservation-conservation ethic. This is at the other end of the spectrum.

"In its extreme, it opposes the use of natural resources as undesirable and to be fought vehemently. Under this approach, waste inputs should be zero. Everything should be in its natural state, even if of no use. It's a swing from the raping and pillage to the fortress mentality."

Prof. Hennigan said there is "a danger of a Mexican standoff" between these extremes and "a creeping paralysis in effectively meeting society's real needs and, at the same time, maintaining reasonable environmental control."

What is needed, he said, is an ecologic-human ethic, which recognizes the primacy of man, his legitimate needs and wants, and the need to reconcile them with the environment.

"The limited capacity of the natural environment to accept insults and the human need for a variety of environmental situations, all of which complement and support life, are part of this concept. Theologically, it is based on stewardship rather than dominion over God's creation."

A public policy based on this middle course would be based on such premises as minimum waste inputs into water; maximum waste treatment; elimination of waste where possible; no introduction of foreign substances into drinking water supplies; increasing tougher standards for streams and effluents; pollution prevention as well as abatement; decisions that favor people ("no more environmental brinkmanship"), and shifting the burden of proof to the polluter rather than the regulatory bodies.

As for the institutions that now govern the Great Lakes, Prof. Hennigan said they are "not the product of any rational design," but what has emerged historically.

"They include federal agencies, a number of states, and literally hundreds of units of local government – a system designed for anarchy and chaos in today's situation." The system is further complicated by its international character.

He called for international policy, planning and administration on the basis of the whole Great Lakes Basin, with a comprehensive water quality management plan.

Although some progress has been made, both in attitudes and programs, "the job remaining to be done staggers the imagination," Prof. Hennigan said. And it won't be done by the use of simplistic slogans like "Dilution is the solution to pollution," or even "Money is the solution to pollution."

He said that in the long run, population control will be the issue on which the future depends. But this offers little hope at present, since no matter what action is taken, the population in the Great Lakes area will increase 50 per cent in the next 30 years.

# Oceans Pollution Seen
# Threat to Climate

SAN FRANCISCO (UPI) – Scientists issued a warning to the human race yesterday that pollution could change the temperature of the oceans and alter the climate of the earth.

E. D. Goldberg, an oceanography chemist, told a meeting of the American Geophysical Union that man is changing his environment almost as much as nature itself.

Goldberg, of the Scripps Institution of Oceanography, La Jolla, Calif., said the effects of pollution are not known but they pose some "haunting" questions.

"Will it alter the ocean as a resource?" he asked. "Will we lose the ocean? There are some complex ecological questions."

Goldberg urged the establishment of monitoring programs to measure the increasing loads of such chemicals as lead, mercury, pesticides and petroleum.

J. O. Fletcher, a physical scientist for the Rand Corp. in Santa Monica, Calif., said man has "only a few decades to solve the problem" of global warming caused by pollution.

"Very substantial changes have taken place during our lifetime," Fletcher said. "There is good evidence that man's influence is small compared to natural ones. However, within another generation, man will become important, the carbon dioxide pollution apparently being the most important."

Carbon dioxide, causing one-third to one-half of the warming in the first part of the 20th century, has had a much greater impact than particulate matter (dust, dirt and smoke), Fletcher said.

## Ice Caps

Global warming could cause further melting of the earth's ice caps and affect its climate.

William W. Kellogg of the National Centre for Atmospheric Research, Boulder, Colo., said the situation points up a problem of educating earthlings that "man has got to change his ways."

Kellogg and Fletcher agreed that population control will be one of the stickiest problems.

"Sooner or later, it (global climate) will have to become a manageable problem," Fletcher said.

*250,000 Tons*

Documenting his assertions of ocean pollution, Goldberg said 250,000 tons of lead drift annually into the oceans of the northern hemisphere. "This compares with the natural leaching in the hemisphere of about 150,000 tons a year," he said. "And we've just been using lead the last 45 years as an anti-knock agent in gasoline."

Goldberg said a million tons of petroleum are introduced to the oceans annually by ships.

"The result has already been felt," he said. "There have been cases of fish tasting of petroleum."

# Scientists Can Start at Beginning in Fight Against Heat Pollution

## Betty Lou Lee

BUFFALO – Thermal or heat pollution may be one type of pollution where the scientists have a head start and aren't faced with trying to undo damage.

Dr. Robert K. Lane, head of the physical limnology section at the Canada Centre for Inland Waters at Burlington, thinks research has started soon enough to seek prevention rather than cure.

"For once in our lives, we have a potential problem," he said yesterday in an interview during the 13th Conference on Great Lakes Research. "We have lots of time to look at it."

He compared the present situation to what could have happened if 50 years ago someone had predicted the 1970 levels of DDT and had set out to see what effect they would have on the environment.

Members of the inland centre have been involved in a study just completed by H. G. Acres Ltd., a consulting firm that surveyed the amount of man-made heat now being poured into the Great Lakes by power plants, sewage treatment plants, steel mills, petroleum refineries and chemical plants, and estimated what these outputs would be by 2000.

Now the problem is to find out what effects these levels are having and will have on the lakes.

"No one has said that in lakes the size of Erie and Ontario thermal input will have a certain effect on the ecology," Dr. Lane said.

"In some small lakes and rivers, it has proven so detrimental that some plants have been closed in the United States . . . but with the Great Lakes, there is a certain amount of disagreement on how this heat is dissipated . . . enough disagreement to undertake a physical study."

Such a study is now underway by a three-man team at the centre, and is expected to be finished in about nine months. They will review all the research that has been done on thermal pollution, use the Acres study data as a basis for quantities of heat involved, and set up a model to study what happens to the heat. Factors to be considered include the effects of current, atmospheric conditions, and at what depths in the lake heated water is discharged.

Once it is known how the heat is spread throughout the lake, it can be determined how much heat added by man will stay in certain areas. Then the biologists can study what effects these levels would have on marine life, both plant and animal.

Dr. Lane said some research has already indicated that algae and plankton growth is stimulated by a rise in water temperature. Sudden changes in temperature of water have also been given as a reason for massive kills of alewives in the Great Lakes.

Additional heat going into the lakes could possibly affect weather, since it would increase evaporation of water. This evaporation probably wouldn't be enough to affect the lake levels, but it could increase snow and rainfall.

Dr. Lane said the centre would work closely with Ontario Hydro and the Ontario Water Resources Commission, which are already doing some studies on power plants along the Great Lakes. "It would be silly of us to duplicate what they're doing, or plunge on by ourselves."

He said the centre also wants to promote research into beneficial uses

of the heated water, such as ice suppression, or keeping sewage lagoons unfrozen. "We'd like to have some engineers look at it, this isn't our bag."

One of the methods of examining heat distribution in the lakes is an infra-red scanner, first developed for military purposes, and used in Vietnam for such things as detecting trucks in a jungle.

Dr. Lane said that by using such a scanner from a plane, a two-dimensional picture of the lake's surface temperature can be obtained that is more detailed than data collected from ships.

It shows heat discharges from power plants and sewage treatment plants.

Because it records energy emitted, rather than energy reflected, as a camera does, it can be used at night.

Dr. Lane said the centre's scanner was used in tests at Chedebucto Bay, N.S., after the Arrow oil spill, to see if it could be useful in detecting oil. At the centre, they are still analyzing the pictures. If it is effective, it could be used to detect oil spills in the Arctic during the months of darkness when cameras or eyes would be useless in surveillance.

# The Common Death
# of a Duck

## Tiny Bennett

A duck, smothered in oil, immobilized and starving, is huddled at the edge of a Toronto beach, awaiting death.

It is a common occurrence, and this bird is one of the many hundreds that will not be picked up, cleaned and restored to health. It is hidden behind a small stone wall, out of sight, and in the chill of the coming night it will die slowly and with no sound to mark its passing.

There is a small pool close by, and in it various kinds of flotsam wash back and forth as small waves ripple in from the lake. It is all so different from the only other place the duck has known – the clean, windswept lands far to the north.

Under the matting oil, if only our eyes could see it, there is the perky, bright form of one of the most noisy and communal of all the diving ducks, a male oldsquaw.

This duck was hatched less than half a year ago in a nest concealed at the base of a clump of dwarf willows, close by a pond set in the Arctic tundra north of the tree-line.

Here in the protective cover, the mother hid the brood from the gulls and skuas that constantly winged over the nesting territory in search of prey. When the day came that she led the ducklings to the pond, several other ducks joined with her to form a convoy of protection.

And there in the land of the midnight sun, the young oldsquaw paddled and learned to dive in the heavily-stained waters of the tundra pond, to snap up aquatic insects and snip off grasses and pondweed.

### Noisy

The oldsquaws are noisy birds, noted for creating a chuckling, incessant chatter. Since the species is among one of the most abundant of the Arctic ducks, there was an almost constant roar as our duck learned to fly above the bleak landscape, and gain strength for the migration to come.

Then as the days grew shorter in that northern land, the migration

urge ran through the noisy throng, and packs of birds lifted, wheeled and headed toward winter quarters.

Some headed south and east to spend winter along the bleak Atlantic coast. Others, of which our duck was one, sped south to the open waters of Lake Ontario.

## Perky Sight

By now the protective dull coloring of summer nesting time had given way to the bright brown and white of winter plumage. The adult males in particular presented a perky sight as, with long thin tails extended, they frolicked in the turbulent air along the passage route.

Resting and feeding in cold, clear silent lakes now feeling the touch of winter's icy fingers, the flocks moved ever south and at last into man's dominion.

In the dawn's gray light the migrating birds jink and flare with alarm at the boom of guns and the red flame lance that stabs upward from long muzzles.

## Protected

That danger passed, the birds come in sight at last of their wintering quarters, the protected lake waters around the Toronto Islands.

The late afternoon sun is glistening from the windows of the downtown buildings and, scudding in low up the wind, the little flock dips and plunges into a smooth slick of oil wastes.

In an instant, the bright feathers are coated with a clogging mess that drips from frantically beating wings and burns eyes like fire.

## Who Knows?

As the ducks struggle the insidious oil smothers the soft down of their bodies, until, disabled, they can do little more than weakly twitch and shake their heads.

Who knows how, where, or when the oil sludge was dumped into the lake?

It might have been an accident, the wrong lever pulled and a tank emptied down a waste pipe rather than channelled into a settling pool. It could be part of the never-ending flow of oil wastes that pours down the Niagara River; it may even be the result of an old dumping from a ship.

Soon the little flock is dispersed and our duck floats low in the water, helpless and carried slowly toward its end behind a small stone wall on a Toronto beach.

In this scientific age, human identification with a wild creature is scorned as anthropomorphic, probably correctly, for it is doubtful if the young duck experienced any great emotion over its fate.

## Common Victim

But it is a victim of water pollution in Lake Ontario, a common victim, for this happens all the time. Maybe it can help us appreciate values that are often played down in favor of the purely scientific approach.

*"It is not possible to find a simpler measure of a good environment than whether fish and wildlife can thrive in it."*

These words by Dr. C. H. D. Clarke, chief of Fish and Wildlife in the Ontario Lands and Forests Department, formed the start of his final paragraph in his paper presented to the Ontario Pollution Control conference in Toronto in December, 1967.

He closed with these words:

"In the fish and wildlife business we know only too well that man was given dominion over the beasts of the fields and the fowl of the air, and we are constantly reminded that he was not given dominion over himself. That is something he has to earn."

In the bright of a chill winter day, a child finds the duck stiff and ugly in death.

And the child weeps, as should all men.

# Sophisticated Oil Pollution Detectors Coming

BUFFALO – Polluters beware. Oil pollution detectors are coming up with equipment just about as sophisticated as the police use to track down criminals.

Take fingerprints, for example. The equivalent of this in the pollution game is a fingerprint of the oil found in water. By identifying the type of oil investigators can trace it back to its source.

Another technique for pinpointing the source of pollution could be compared to the police techniques used on a scrap of car paint that will identify the make and model. By analyzing the oil it again can be traced to its source.

These techniques were outlined yesterday at the 13th Conference on Great Lakes Research. The fingerprinting technique was described by W. Dewitt Johnson and F. D. Fuller of the Federal Water Pollution Control Administration in Chicago. Since different types of oil have different ratios of sulphur and phosphorus, by analyzing this ratio in oil found in water the type of oil can be identified.

This isn't useful or even needed in large oil spills from tankers, such as that at Chedebucto Bay, N.S. In these cases it's obvious where the oil is coming from.

But some rivers, lakes and streams get oil from a number of sources – ships pumping bilge, commercial and industrial plants, domestic sewage and storm runoffs. It can be bunker oil, fuel oil, vegetable oil, industrial grade oils, or simply the oil that's washed off parking lots in the rain.

The second analyzing method was described by F. K. Kawahara of the Federal Water Pollution Control Administration, Cincinnatti, and it uses oily materials found in the bottom mud. It runs tests on factors like their boiling point, solubility and density, to identify where they came from.

Ronald I. Frank, research physicist at Cornell Aeronautical Laboratory Inc., who chaired the session, said in an interview that there are

10,000 oil spills a year in the United States and only a few of these are as easily traced as a major tanker spill.

In the Buffalo area his firm is operating a government-financed program to both prevent and then eliminate oil pollution in an area that has, among other industries, an oil refinery, a steel mill, a chemical plant and a soft drink plant.

They are using surface barriers like booms to contain surface oil. Underwater barriers that won't interfere with shipping are also being tested. A pipe is placed on the bottom and compressed air is blown through holes in the pipe. As bubbles rise, they drag water with them, creating a counter-flow on the surface that traps oil in a stagnant area and prevents it being carried along with the normal flow. It can then be skimmed off this area.

The project also includes monitors in the sewer system to detect what types of oil are passing through. Studies will also be done to see how it can be trapped in the system and not expelled into waterways.

A Buffalo company may have come up with a material that will help in future oil spills like that in Nova Scotia. It's a polymer that makes a layer between oil and water, thickens the oil and prevents it from spreading. It acts as a sort of corral to keep the oil in one spot so it can be removed from the water.

Karl Moeglich of the Zaremba Company said the material had been tested on Bunker C oil, the type spilled in Chedebucto Bay, and it made the oil 100 times as thick.

The polymer reduces spreading by interfering with the adhesion between oil and water.

# Mercury Spills
# in More Rivers

MONTREAL – Three Canadian companies admitted yesterday they are discharging mercury into the St. Lawrence, St. Maurice and Saguenay Rivers.

But spokesmen for all three – Aluminum Co. of Canada Ltd., Canadian Industries Ltd., and Standard Chemical Co., Ltd. – said they do not believe the amount of pollution is dangerous and added that they have taken measures to reduce mercury discharge to the smallest amounts possible.

Meanwhile it was announced in Columbus, Ohio, that the state will

The Spectator

DOUG WRIGHT

"No, I don't like mercury......but I'm not that crazy about fishermen either!"

sue a Canadian-based company and an American firm to recover damages caused by mercury pollution of Lake Erie.

The news came a day after the state's ban on all commercial fishing on the Ohio side of Lake Erie until the extent of an investigation into mercury pollution can be determined.

Attorney General Paul W. Brown of Ohio said he expects adjoining states to join Ohio in the filing of actions against Dow Chemical Co., of Sarnia, Ontario and the Wyandotte Chemical Co., of Detroit.

Brown said U.S. government tests show mercury traces in fish which exceed safety limits.

And at London, Ontario, biologist Nervald Fimreite of the University of Western Ontario announced that some Lake St. Clair fish tested for mercury contamination showed higher readings than fish that killed people in Japan in the 1960's.

At Windsor, Dr. Joseph R. Jones, director of the Essex county health unit, said about 40 residents who had been tested for mercury could know by this weekend if they had actually consumed mercury. Samples from heavy fish eaters and non-fish eaters are being examined in the provincial health laboratory in Toronto.

# Dow Won't Compensate Fishermen

TORONTO – The president of Dow Chemical of Canada Ltd. has denied his company's responsibility to compensate Lake St. Clair fishermen whose livelihoods have been destroyed by mercury pollution.

His denial of financial responsibility followed Dow's admission yesterday that the company was a source of mercury pollution in St. Clair waters.

However, Federal Resources Minister J. J. Greene and Ontario Resources Minister George Kerr have made it plain that those responsible for polluting Ontario's waterways ultimately must pay.

After announcing federal-provincial "social measure" loans to persons affected by the pollution, Mr. Greene made it clear the loans are not grants against future compensation nor compensation in any way.

Both Mr. Kerr and Mr. Greene suggested suits for civil liability will have to be launched by injured parties if there is an ultimate refusal by industry to pay compensation.

L. D. Smithers, Dow president, told the federal and provincial officials at a Queen's Park meeting that his company does not believe it is the only source of mercury pollution on the Detroit–St. Clair rivers system.

Nor does it believe mercury pollution alone is responsible for contamination of the area's fish, he said.

A federal ban last week on sale and export of fish taken from the system was blamed on mercury poisoning.

The company plans to conduct its own engineering surveys of Lake St. Clair and the St. Clair River, and has agreed to stop mercury leaks within its Sarnia plant and stop mercury from escaping into the Great Lakes.

Mr. Smithers indicated the studies will take as long as is necessary to produce a result.

The apparent direct loss to the 65 to 70 commercial fishermen operating on Lake St. Clair, with a catch last year of 1,000,000 pounds, is estimated at about $1,000,000 if the fisheries can be opened up again for the 1971 season.

# Polluters Are Thieves: Kerr

**Bas Korstanje**

TORONTO – In a rare display of fury and energy Resources Minister George Kerr yesterday accused industry of being "the thief" in the Great Lakes pollution crisis.

He also said that as far as he was concerned compensation will be paid for the losses to fishermen.

Waving his fist, the minister shouted that Lake St. Clair had been polluted for 20 years.

"Industry knows about it and if they have got any conscience at all, they will start cleaning up," he said.

The angry outburst came in the middle of an emotion-charged emergency debate in the Ontario Legislature on the fishing industry in Lakes St. Clair and Erie.

It was sparked by opposition accusations that the responsibility for the pollution crisis lay with the government.

"Industry is the polluter in this case, not the government. Remember that," Mr. Kerr said.

Over the shouted interjections from Liberal and NDP members, Mr. Kerr roared: "Industry is the thief. We are the policemen. Industry does it. You control."

Constantly heckled, Mr. Kerr continued: "We will do our part, but we are sick and tired of trying to be Sherlock Holmes. We will continue to play the detective, but we want to think that we are dealing with responsible people, just as concerned as we are about the environment of this province.

"The people who run industry in this province live in this province. Therefore they should have just the same amount of interest as any government agency."

Although he had earlier stated that the matter of compensation would be decided at a meeting with federal officials scheduled for today, he said that as far as he was concerned compensation for losses would be paid.

The Ottawa meeting originally was to be held yesterday, but was postponed after a special flight to Ottawa had been cancelled because of the weather.

Mr. Kerr told the legislature that the Ontario Water Resources Commission had done everything possible to avoid and stop pollution of the lakes.

He said that as a result of normal "policing" the OWRC received in May, 1969, a spot sample taken in Lake St. Clair containing mercury. He said it was not until August, 1969, that high levels of mercury in the sample were confirmed.

He said when the report came out the source of the pollution was pinpointed in Sarnia, where an inventory was taken at the Dow Chemical Plant, which proved that mercury was being discharged.

Immediate efforts were made to eliminate the source of the pollution, he said.

# Private Phosphate Probe Follows Gov't 'Secret'

## John Gibson

An anti-pollution group in Toronto has conducted its own investigation into the phosphate content of 65 detergents because the government has failed to publish official statistics, it was disclosed yesterday.

Bryan Kelly, of the University of Toronto's Pollution Probe, said in an interview the group's findings will be made public this weekend.

He charged the government has kept the figures secret because of pressure from the detergent companies.

"Apparently the government has done an analysis of the detergent, but if they release the results they become *prima facie* evidence," he said.

The 22-year-old zoology graduate, who works full time for Pollution Probe, said the group was unsuccessful in an attempt to get federal figures for comparison.

He said Pollution Probe's list will show phosphate contents ranging from 52 per cent to 18 per cent in heavy-duty detergents and similar variations in other categories.

The statistics will first be made public Sunday night on the CBC television program Weekend, he said.

Earlier, Mr. Kelly testified before the Hamilton hearing of the International Joint Commission on pollution in the Great Lakes.

Two advisory boards to the commission have urged that phosphate-based detergents be banned by 1972.

Phosphates promote algae growth, which clogs the lakes and uses up vital oxygen as it decays.

In detergents, phosphorus is the ingredient that holds dirt in suspension in water so that it does not stick to clothes.

Mr. Kelly told the Commission: "We believe that, contrary to what the detergent manufacturers think, many customers are concerned with the (phosphate) problem and want to do something.

"We will provide them with the missing information and allow them to react as they will – perhaps by switching to soaps or low-phosphate detergents."

# 10% of Cottages Pollute Lakes: Task Force

Tough new measures to prevent pollution of Ontario's recreational waters have been recommended to the Ontario Government in the report of a task force.

One of the steps, placing all land in the province under subdivision control, has already been taken because of the report, which was completed in March but made public only yesterday.

The report estimates that 10 per cent of the existing 140,000 to 200,000 cottages in the province are contributing to water pollution, and 11,000 more cottages are going up each year.

In addition to the new subdivision legislation, the report has prompted the Government to launch a major program this summer to find and correct pollution sources in the Kawartha Lakes, considered by provincial officials to require priority action.

But the report argues that an intensive investigation and correction program is only part of the answer to rehabilitating lakes in cottage areas and preventing pollution problems as new cottages are built.

"Only a major revision of the present control system will achieve the desired results," the report says.

New controls which are urged include:

– A requirement that every municipality have a building bylaw so that no building can be erected without a permit;

– Regulations requiring the approval of the local Medical Officer of Health before a building permit is issued when a lot is not serviced by municipal water and sewer facilities;

– Provincial regulations setting out minimum standards for private sewage disposal systems, and requiring municipalities to establish sewage haulage systems when cottages are required to have sewage holding tanks;

– A minimum lot size of one acre as a guideline for cottage development approval in the Precambrian Shield area and a minimum of half an acre elsewhere when water and sewage disposal services will be contained on the lot;

– A ban on development for any unserviced lot that is "topographically incapable (with too little soil or drainage) of sustaining on-site sewage disposal adequate for full-time occupancy";

– Giving health department inspectors authority to enter private property and enforce pollution regulations, and to issue correction orders or closing orders, subject to appropriate appeal and review procedures;

– Licensing of all fishing huts or other structures erected on lakes and rivers, with licensees subject to regulations covering removal of buildings and disposal of wastes.

The report says the recommended changes in legislation and procedures "are designed to strengthen the entire program involving cottage developments to minimize pollution."

In addition to the specific changes, the report asks the Cabinet to prepare an over-all plan for the development of recreational areas in the province.

The report also says there is a lack of information about the capacity of specific lakes to sustain recreational activities, and it urges a study program to develop criteria by which lakes could be classified as a basis for development planning.

The studies should take into account not only the direct effect of cottage development, the report says, but also such things as oil and noise pollution from boats.

Another recommendation is that the Government prepare guideline booklets for the public and for land developers explaining the significance of environmental factors, steps that can be taken to protect the environment, and procedures that should be followed in selecting land for development.

The report says there has been a general assumption by developers, municipalities and some local health authorities that 15,000 square feet is adequate where sewage and water facilities will have to be on-site, and 7,500 square feet where one service will be supplied by a municipal system.

Those figures have been used as a standard "regardless of the soil or topographic conditions or the extent of existing or proposed development," the report adds.

It recommends a new standard of one acre – 43,560 square feet – where either sewage or water supply facilities or both have to be supplied on the lot if the land is in the Precambrian Shield area, and half an acre in other areas.

Any reduction from those requirements, the report says, should have to be supported by an engineering report establishing the adequacy of the smaller area.

"It should be further recognized that in particular instances larger areas than those recommended may be necessary, and in other cases no development should be permitted."

Some local health authorities are at present recommending approval of development on lots on the basis of pit privies when there is insufficient soil to install a septic tank system, the report says, but "it is well known that most cottagers will eventually change from pit privies to an indoor flush toilet system."

It is this situation which prompts the recommendation that no unserviced lot be approved for development unless the topography will permit sewage disposal facilities adequate for full-time cottage occupancy.

As an interim policy for this year pending preparation of an over-all development policy, the report recommends that health authorities refuse approval of all cottage development where soil conditions would allow only pit privies and not septic tanks.

The report says present legislation does not give health department officials the power to enter private premises, to issue orders for necessary corrective work, or to order the closing of premises if the work is not done.

The report says these powers are essential to investigate and correct pollution in cottage areas.

The report was prepared by officials of the provincial departments of Energy and Resources Management, Health, Lands and Forests and Municipal Affairs, and the Ontario Water Resources Commission.

Despite its statement that the new control powers are needed immediately, Government sources indicated yesterday that further legislation is unlikely to be introduced before the House adjourns later this week for a summer recess.

# Why Lakes Become Green and Slimy

## H. B. N. Hynes

As a scientist who has for many years been concerned with the biological problems caused by water pollution, I am often asked by anxious cottage-owners what they should do to prevent their lakes from becoming all green and slimy and "dead like Lake Erie." In the course of these conversations I have become aware that there are many misconceptions and much misinformation about what does occur when a lake becomes altered by human activity. The topic is fairly complex, but the general principles are clear enough to explain fairly simply.

*Water-filled Hole*

Basically there are about a dozen general points about plants, animals and lakes that have to be grasped:

(1) A lake is a water-filled hole caused by some geological accident such as gouging out by ice, blocking of a valley by a landslide or a moraine, or even by a dam. It fills with water by drainage from the surrounding land directly, and usually also via streams, and most of the precipitation falling on to the watershed either reaches the lake or is evaporated. However, in areas where the rocks are porous a fair amount may percolate down into the water-table, and some or all of this may never reach the lake.

This would be unusual in Ontario's cottage country, where the rocks are mostly hard and crystalline.

(2) Most lakes have an outflow stream, but from some the water leaves by seepage into the water-table or through a moraine. In dry areas, such as the Prairies, the rate of evaporation may be so high that the basin never fills to overflowing, and the lake becomes steadily saltier as it retains everything that comes in except the water. Where there is outflow or seepage most of the salts go out again in solution.

(3) The inflowing water brings in silt, twigs, dead leaves and other debris, and this all settles out in the basin and slowly fills it, so all lakes disappear in time. In fact most of them last only for a few, or a few

tens of, thousands of years, and the reason that we now have so many in Canada is the recent geological activity of the Ice Age. In areas, such as the central and southern United States, where no recent large geological cataclysm has occurred, natural lakes are rare.

(4) Any activity in the watershed of a lake that causes soil erosion greatly increases the rate of filling up, and almost everything men do, including building, plowing, clearing the forest and making roads, belongs in that category.

## Dissolves Everything

(5) Water is a very strange material and has properties that it shares with few other liquids. Not only will it dissolve almost everything, but it becomes lighter when it freezes (ice floats but almost everything else sinks when it becomes cold enough to freeze) and it is at its densest when it is at 4 degrees Centigrade (39.2 degrees Fahrenheit) and becomes lighter when it is warmer or colder than this (other liquids become denser as they get colder). These thermal properties have the very important consequence that ice forms on the surface of lakes and has much warmer water (up to 39.2 degrees Fahrenheit) a few inches below it. Also the surface water in a deep lake warms up in summertime. This, being less dense, lies on top of a layer of denser, much cooler water. The result is a thermal discontinuity at a certain depth – we call it a thermocline – above which the water is stirred and circulated by the wind and below which it has no contact with the air all summer long. Just how deep the thermocline lies depends on a number of things, but generally speaking it is deeper in larger and more exposed lakes than in small or sheltered ones. Somewhere between 20 and 40 feet would be fairly typical for many lakes in Ontario's cottage country.

(6) Plants and algae, which are just microscopic plants, grow by using the energy of light to convert carbon dioxide and water into organic matter, but they also need the so-called nutrient salts to incorporate into necessary organic compounds. The three most important of these are nitrate and phosphate and potassium. The others, which include iron, calcium and magnesium, are needed in much lesser amounts, and as they are usually amply available in natural water, they do not concern us further here. Any particular species of plant needs the three principal nutrients in a fairly definite ratio, so a shortage of any one of them (or of carbon dioxide or water) limits its growth, and addition of more of the limiting nutrient increases growth, but addition of more of the others has little effect.

(7) On land any one of the three may be limiting to certain plants – we fertilize fruit trees with potassium and lawns with nitrate – but in lake water phosphate is the most usual culprit, and addition of phosphate nearly always enhances algal growth. Where, however, algae are already very dense the plants may run out of carbon dioxide, or bicarbonate (limestone in solution) which they can also use, or light as they shade one another out. But by that stage the lake is already in a poor way.

(8) The reasons why phosphate is the most usual limiting factor in fresh water are complex, but with some oversimplification we can say that it is relatively scarce anyway and, unlike the other two, on land it is tightly bound into the soil so it does not leach out so readily. About as much nitrate and potassium leave a lake via the outflow as leach into it, but phosphate, which mostly comes in on soil particles and dead leaves etc., remains in the lake. This is because it is very rapidly taken up by bacteria and plants, even far in excess of their immediate needs, and because, as in soil, it readily becomes bound into the mud when oxygen is present.

When oxygen is absent the phosphate is released again and is rapidly taken up by the algae, and when they die and decay it is released again to be recycled again and again, so it is effectively trapped in the lake. The fact that the phosphate is bound into the soil points up the significance of soil erosion, and the thermal properties of water insure that twice in each year the mud and overlying water are cut off from the atmosphere – below the ice and below the thermocline. It will be clear therefore that twice in each year there is a risk of deoxygenation at the mud-water interface if there is a great deal of organic matter to decay.

(9) Water at normal temperatures dissolves a little oxygen, about 0.1 per cent by volume, which is enough for aquatic animals. It gets it either from the atmosphere or from the plants and algae growing in it. In fact the ultimate source of all oxygen is from growing plants; they produce it, they do not use it up as I have heard some people assert about algae. So, active growth of algae results in more oxygen in the water, and in summer well-fertilized lakes give it off to the atmosphere. However, when plants die and decay, or are eaten and digested, or are prevented from growing by lack of light, they can ultimately use up the same amount of oxygen as they produced when they were growing, and they also once more release into circulation the nutrient salts and the carbon dioxide they had taken up. Eating and digestion go on all the

time everywhere, and some use of oxygen by living plants occurs every night.

However, in the dark of winter under the ice, and in summer below the thermocline, oxygen is progressively used up all the time and it cannot be replenished from the atmosphere. Therefore, in a lake which grows a lot of algae because it is well fertilized, there tends to be de-oxygenation in winter under the ice – remember it is relatively warm there so decay goes on all the time. Similarly, in the summer in the deep dark layers below the thermocline decaying algae abound in enriched lakes and the supply of oxygen is soon exhausted.

(10) Deoxygenation has two consequences. It suffocates animals, for example the winter-kill of fish, and it releases phosphate much more readily from the mud. It therefore escalates the effects of enrichment with phosphate. That is why lakes so often suddenly begin to produce offensive blooms of algae after many years of apparently satisfactory occupation by cottagers. Slowly over the years the fertility is built up, and then the critical point is attained when, during the winter, or below the thermocline in the summer, the oxygen content of the water at the mud-water interface falls to a level low enough to release large amounts of locked in phosphate.

Then when the water again mixes freely, at the thaw or in the fall, it all comes welling up and the algae bloom enormously. That is almost a point of no return as the system is self-sustaining – more algae, less oxygen near the mud, more phosphate, more algae and so on. Of course this cycle may not lope into an unfaltering stride from the start; a short winter, a late spring or an early fall may check it for a year, or even two or three, but once begun it is on its way and we have no effective means of checking it.

To prevent any further addition of phosphate would help, hence all the fuss about detergents; and in time, presumably, enough would be lost from the system, through the outflow and perhaps deep into the mud, to break the cycle. But we really have no idea how long "in time" may be; we do know that ominously lake mud in general equilibrium with the water normally contains about 1,000 times as much phosphate as the water, so enriched mud can fertilize a great deal of water. Actually, of course, there is usually much more water than mud, and there are indications that only the upper layers of mud are able to give up their phosphate. But there is some uncertainty about this and the mud is usually many feet deep. Twenty feet is not uncommon in Southern Ontario.

(11) Finally, the average cottager wants not only to boat and swim in water that is free of algae blooms and dense growths of blanket weed, he also likes to fish, and here again excessive enrichment works against him. Theoretically, and actually in practice also, extra fertilization leads to more plant growth, and this to more insects, worms, etc. for fish to eat and hence to more production of fish. That is fine, up to a point. Indeed unproductive lakes have often been fertilized with phosphate and other nutrients to increase their yield of fish, and the fish-farmers of Asia and Africa add all kinds of materials to their ponds to increase production.

*Prized Lake Fish*

Unfortunately, however, from our point of view here, beyond that certain point the production is of the wrong kind. Our most prized lake fish is the trout, which does best in nutrient-poor waters. Trout also cannot stand high temperatures, so in summer they retreat into the cool water below the thermocline. But once the lake is sufficiently enriched for the water there to be seriously deoxygenated they are between the Scylla of high temperature and the Charybdis of suffocation, and that

soon puts an end to them. Similarly bass and the sunfish thrive best in reasonably rich water, but as the fertility increases and algae become more common they are replaced first by perch and then by suckers and carp. People then say that the lake is dead. It isn't of course; it is more alive than it has ever been in terms of production of algae, insects and fish but they are all of the wrong kind. The algae float in unsightly scum, blanket weed coats submerged objects, clouds of (non-biting, but nasty) midges emerge, and fat suckers and carp wallow in the soup. Moreover, it smells unpleasant and real estate values plummet.

How can the cottager prevent this from happening? The simple answer is not to go there at all and to leave the lake in its pristine beauty, but the next best thing is to appreciate fully the principles outlined above and act accordingly.

Do not clear vegetation beyond absolute necessity nor do anything else that causes soil erosion.

Do not introduce fertilizers into the watershed – to make, for instance, that lakeside lawn nice and green; it will make the lake green also.

Do not deposit garbage, or bury it, anywhere inside the watershed, nor feel that a cesspool or a soakaway pit is the answer to the sewage disposal problem. Remember that all organic matter is originally plant material and that as those plants grew they took up nutrient salts from the soil. This applies to the tree that was made into a cardboard box, the grass eaten by the steer that provided the steak and the potato you ate with it. So when they decay, or are digested, the nutrient salts are again released, but now they are in the watershed.

## Deterioration Begins

Sooner or later, then, as urine or by flushing or seepage, they will probably get into the lake, and the insidious deterioration has begun. The only answer is to deposit nothing that was brought from outside in the watershed, to carry out the garbage and pipe out or pump out the sewage. This costs money, but then so did the lot and the cottage, and the lake that is treated with respect in this way will probably last for generations while many of the rest will probably be ruined before the end of the century. Think what that will do to the real estate value of the wise and cautious cottager!

A final and most pressing question. What can we do for the lakes which are already at or approaching the point of no return? This is a difficult one. In the United States, one enterprising real estate agent bought up lake areas which had been abandoned because of their burgeoning fertility, removed the mud which was harboring the phosphate, put in a ring sewer, rebuilt the cottages, sold them, and pumped the sewage over – to another watershed one supposes. Another possible solution, under investigation in my laboratory, is to lay polythene sheeting over the whole bed of the lake, thus sealing in the phosphate, and thereafter adhering rigidly to the rules set out above. I understand that some enterprising firms already manufacture swimming pools to be sunk in lakes; maybe they could be persuaded by a consortium of cottage owners to make something larger.

# Part C

# The Soiled Earth

# Pitfalls in
# New Mining Plans

## Stan McNeill

Many an Ontario municipality must have breathed a quiet sigh of
relief recently when the provincial government announced it was clamp-
ing down on the operations of all quarries and pits.

Nasty things, these pits, especially when they're cluttering up your
backyard, polluting the landscape and shattering the calm with dust
and noise; more especially when your bylaws seldom have the teeth to
deal with the problems and headaches they cause.

So it appeared to be a godsend when Mines Minister Allan Lawrence
came along with his proposal for a take-over of all surface mining
operations.

Instead of mining companies having the right to plunder the land
wherever they chose, they would first have to come to terms with the
mines department; instead of operators being allowed to work around
the clock, six days a week, hours would be regulated by Mr. Lawrence
and his trusty men.

And best of all, instead of being able to walk away and leave the
landscape gouged and scarred when pits were worked out, companies
would be required to rehabilitate the sites and restore them to some
type of land-use.

At first glance the proposals looked good and most municipalities
were ready to accept them.

But in the few weeks since the plans were introduced no fewer than
23 municipalities have lodged objections, causing Mines Minister
Lawrence to delay implementation for four months.

Why the sudden change of heart?

Mostly it can be traced to one man, Clark Muirhead, a councillor for
Uxbridge Township, who went through the proposals with a fine-tooth
comb and saw in them an open invitation to mining companies to
ravage the countryside whenever and wherever they saw fit.

It was Mr. Muirhead who persuaded his fellow councillors to circu-
late a resolution to all Ontario municipalities, pointing out the pitfalls

he saw in the proposed legislation and calling for a halt to its implementation.

His strategy may not work in the end but at least it has provided a breathing spell for councils to take a fresh look at the proposals.

And there's some interesting reading in them. For instance, municipalities will have the power under official plans and zoning bylaws to restrict quarry and pit sites, or ban them altogether. But get this: The province's chief mining engineer (who comes under the department of mines) will have the power to reject or order changes in site plans.

In effect this gives the department pre-emptive powers in all matters of land-use. Even the municipal affairs department will have to take second place.

Taking this to its broadest conclusion it means that a person owning property in Ontario – a cottage, farm, home or land – could be subject to the mines department staking it out as suitable for the mining industry and having it entered as such on subsequent official plans. Perhaps that appears a little drastic, and chances are it would never happen. But under the proposed legislation it could.

Superficially, proposals in the report promise a much better deal for Ontario residents than they ever had before – especially in the matter of cleaning up worked-out stone quarries and gravel pits.

But the document is so loosely worded that it would be almost impossible to take it too seriously. It's littered with such phrases as "where possible," "where practicable," "where desirable," "as often as necessary," "as far as is practicable," and "may" – phrases that undermine any serious intent in the plans.

The danger that some see in the proposed legislation is that it gives far too much power to the mines department – the very department whose task it is to promote the production of sand and gravel.

That's something like putting phosphate makers in charge of pollution control. Or, in the words of Mr. Muirhead, like asking the Mafia to help re-draft the Criminal Code.

It's apparent that the department and the aggregate producers make a good team. In 1950 production of sand, stone and gravel in Ontario was a mere 2,000,000 tons. Last year it had risen to 50,000,000 tons, and the forecast for 1980 is 90,000,000 tons.

The materials are widespread throughout southern Ontario but because transportation is a major element in the cost, mining tends to be concentrated around Toronto, Hamilton, Brantford and Paris.

No one is denying that without a large, convenient supply of stone, sand and gravel, construction in Ontario would be in a mess. And for their parts in the current boom the mining companies get full marks.

But their methods in the past have never exactly endeared them to the public. Too often have they ripped open the countryside, leaving it brutally gouged, perhaps forever; too often have they stripped the land of its wealth, unmindful of the future, leaving unsightly gaping holes – a rash of giant pock-marks fit only for the dumping of garbage and the growing of weeds; too often has there been the day- and night-long sound of crushers and loaders, audible at two miles in any direction, and clouds of dust that leave a filmy brown coat on everything for miles around.

Add to that the huge 40-ton trucks that tear up the surface of country roads, and often present a very real hazard to local motorists, and the extent of the problem becomes apparent.

Fortunately, not all mining companies can be tarred with the same brush, and not all disused quarries and pits are left to become dangerous eyesores. Hamilton's Royal Botanical Gardens were once a gravel pit. At the Belfountain Conservation area on the Credit River part of a former quarry is now a swimming pool. And former gravel pits at Lobo, west of London, and Maple Honeypot, near Maple, have been transformed into a trout pool and ski area respectively.

Obviously an abandoned quarry need not be left to rot if enough people care – but first and foremost it should be the responsibility of those who created the mess in the first place.

The trouble is, up to now too many companies have been all too ready to wash their hands of the business once they have worked it for all it's worth, and to let other people worry about what's left.

They can afford to. By the time the scale of operations had started to produce real and widespread nuisance, the industry was so well dug in, so rich and powerful politically, that it could ignore the public's complaints and ride roughshod over the bylaws of small municipalities.

Uxbridge Township found that out to its cost only a couple of months ago when the Ontario Supreme Court quashed a bylaw which would have limited operations in the township to 12 hours a day instead of 24, and to five days a week instead of six, ruling the bylaw prohibitive rather than regulatory.

"Mining companies today have the 19th century robber-baron mentality," Muirhead says. "They plunder the land and don't give a damn for anyone or anything."

Uxbridge Township, less than 50 miles north of Toronto, is a good example of what could happen in other parts of the province if the proposed legislation goes through without amendments.

At present in the township there are about 45 gravel pits, operated by 30 mining companies. "We're the gravel pit capital of the world," says Muirhead.

He says that some 4,500 acres, about 10 per cent of the township's acreage, are owned by gravel interests. And once-beautiful countryside is beginning to look like a "lunar landscape."

It is these gravel interests that are responsible for the proposed provincial legislation, Muirhead charges. "Fearing that one of the key territories in their empire was about to become subject to some law, regulation and order, with the passing by Uxbridge Township of a comprehensive official plan, zoning bylaw and gravel pit bylaw, the gravel people got together in the back room of the mines department at Queen's Park with some of the civil service from that and other departments, and came up with a proposed new deal for themselves."

It is their recommendations, he says, that are contained in the Report of the Industrial Minerals Committee, on which Mines Minister Lawrence based his proposed legislation.

Muirhead is the first to admit that he has a personal axe to grind. He moved to Uxbridge a few years ago to find peace and quiet, and found himself surrounded by noise and confusion and dirt.

He is also the first to admit that a provincial take-over is the best thing that could happen – provided everyone were given a fair shake. As it stands, he says, the proposed legislation is merely giving mining companies the undisputed right to plunder the land.

With the future of the Niagara Escarpment hanging in the balance, municipalities in this area probably will be taking a second, harder look at Mr. Lawrence's proposals.

Any mistakes now could prove very costly in future years.

# Pollution Hitting
# the Hothouse?

## Nick Fillmore

HALIFAX – Premier G. I. Smith said in the Nova Scotia Legislature this week that the Nova Scotia Power Commission is investigating allegations that pollutants from a power commission industrial stack in Pictou County killed greenhouse produce in the area.

Willis Mackeen, a Pictou County greenhouse operator, said he has suffered major losses in his operation from periodic overdoses of sulphur dioxide, one of the more deadly pollutants from industrial stacks.

Killed during the past seven months has been Mr. Mackeen's entire crop of carnations and 2,700 rose bushes. Damage is estimated in excess of $10,000, He has also been told by horticulturists that he will be unable to produce tomatoes, snapdragons, roses, lettuce or carnations – the bread and butter crops of the provincial greenhouse industry.

Tests are being carried out to determine the exact source of the air pollution. Two nearby industrial plants are operated by Scott Maritimes Pulp Ltd. and the Government-owned Nova Scotia Power Commission.

Dr. Gordon Ogden, an environmental biologist at Dalhousie University here, said he is convinced that rose leaves from Mr. Mackeen's nursery he has examined show "classical sulphur dioxide damage." Tests he has conducted on the spot show concentrations of sulphur dioxide consistently in the range of .2 parts per million, with reading heights of .46 parts per million when the wind is blowing from the power commission plant.

"The sulphur dioxide has to be coming from the stacks," he said.

The levels reached are believed to be well above safe minimums in New York City, according to Dr. Ogden. When sulphur dioxide reaches a level of .2 ppm, officials there expect "several hundred additional deaths that day."

The only area of Nova Scotia with any form of air pollution regulations is Halifax, which has only a smoke stack ordinance. However, a spokesman for the Department of Health said he anticipates legislation to protect the province from growing industrial pollution within two years. "We've been pushing the Government with no luck," said C. E. Tupper, director of the environmental hygiene division of the Department of Health. "But the way things are changing we expect the Government will soon start pushing us."

# Weed-killer Still Used Here

## Peter Calamai

OTTAWA – A common weed-killer, banned in the U.S. yesterday because of possible thalidomide-like effects, is still allowed in Canadian homes and farms despite the protests of federal health officials.

Officials of the federal food and drug directorate are up in arms today because federal agriculture pesticide experts ignored their warnings about the weed-killer last December.

Small amounts of the herbicide – called 2-4-5-T – have been proven to cause gross birth malformations and death to mice and rats in recent independent Canadian and U.S. experiments.

The malformations caused when the chemical is included in food given pregnant rats and mice include blindness in 30 per cent of the cases, diseased kidneys, cleft palates and facial deformities.

"They look more like pups; they don't even look like rats," Dr. Alec Morrison, deputy director-general of the food and drug directorate, said last night.

A joint announcement yesterday by the U.S. departments of health, agriculture and the interior in Washington said two uses of the herbicide are suspended immediately and two other uses will be cancelled as soon as possible.

Suspended immediately in the U.S. were uses of 2-4-5-T in liquid form for weed control in home-and-garden products and for spraying of lakes and ponds. Under threat of cancellation are the use of the chemical in dry form in home-and-garden products and for food crops.

About 43,000 acres in Western Canada was sprayed with the herbicide last year, mostly to control hemp nettles in wheat, oats and barley. The herbicide is also registered for use in Canada as a turf treatment on home lawns and golf courses.

Canadian National Railways and several provincial hydro companies have admitted that 2-4-5-T is used in regular weed control programs along their rights-of-way.

A U.S. review of pesticides warned in December that immediate checks should be made on mothers who may have been exposed to 2-4-5-T as a result of farm work, accidental ingestion or industrial exposure.

Dr. Morrison said the food and drug directorate has urged the federal agriculture department to immediately ban the use of the chemical on the three cereal crops.

"We've also told agriculture that we think it should not be used in circumstances where it might drift onto food supplies or over water used for drinking," he said.

A food and drug spokesman said detailed studies so far – about 50 samples taken from wheat crops near Winnipeg in late December – had not detected any residues of the herbicide in the grain.

"I don't think we'll find any in the food chain," said Dr. Morrison. "There's a built-in safety factor because it is applied when the wheat is very young."

# Part D

# Chemical Warfare

*The evidences of chemicals as a major cause of deterioration of our soil, water, and air resources have been well documented. Wildlife, vegetation and recreational areas have been affected also. With some surprise, Canadians have become aware that chemicals such as DDT have not been as beneficial to mankind as was originally claimed.*

*DDT, the miracle preventer of malaria, was first developed for insect control in tropical zones. Its use spread rapidly into temperate climates, and became very extensive during the 1950s as part of forest management practices for large timber tracts in Canada. In this later aspect it*

*appears to have been misused, and Canadians have seen their wildlife
resources seriously affected as a result.*

*Similar charges are made against other insecticides, fertilizers, and
phosphates with their various uses. Yet, we need to be careful in allowing
our concern to develop into wholesale condemnation. Wise use of DDT
has been beneficial. Widespread criticism of phosphates in detergents has
resulted in a substantial reduction in their use, but not all Canadian
scientists agree that phosphates are the real culprit in water pollution. It
is recognized that the practice of salting major roads and highways during the winter helps to reduce the amount of road ice, and aids in snow
removal. On the other hand, road salt is expensive to apply, promotes
rapid rusting of automobiles, and is contributing to the pollution of fresh
water lakes. Despite these problems, the official view held by provincial
authorities is that the use of road salt in winter is necessary and that
the benefits outweigh the disadvantages.*

*The articles in this section present both sides of this issue. Modern
technology has made the use of chemicals a part of the Canadian way of
life but wise management is needed to ensure that they do not become
a part of its destruction.*

# Pesticide Pollution
# Could Be Cut in Half,
# Zoologist Says

Pesticide pollution of our environment would be cut in half if the chemicals were used discriminately in forestry and agriculture, a leading
Toronto zoologist said Saturday.

Dr. D. A. Chant, U of T zoology department chairman and active
member of Pollution Probe and Group Action to Stop Pollution, said
50 percent of pesticides used are unnecessary.

# To DDT or Not to DDT

## John Flanders

The Association of Allied Leaf Eaters and Livestock Pests is having the last laugh on the Ontario government – and the consumer.

In fact, the 1,000 insect families that form the association and cause damage to Canadian crops and livestock are having a picnic to celebrate the government's ban on DDT.

Their mirth, it seems, originates from the heavy restrictions placed on the use of DDT Jan. 1.

Other insecticides will be permitted, but almost all of the alternatives to DDT are more costly and researchers say they will undoubtedly produce an increase in food production costs. And it's clear that the consumer will foot the bill.

Under regulations announced by Health Minister Thomas Wells, DDT will be permitted only to protect tobacco crops from cutworm damage; limit plant bug damage to apple trees and control bats, when used by licensed structural exterminators. Purchasers and vendors were placed under strict control.

On the federal level, authorities will sanction use of DDT for insect control only in emergencies and its use will be restricted to 12 agricultural crops, thereby cutting down its use by an anticipated 90 per cent.

Prime Minister Trudeau, in making the announcement, noted that there is evidence of environmental pollution from DDT, especially among fish and birds. And he said that while there was no injury to humans from the pesticide buildup, there also was a lack of clear-cut evidence about the long-term effects.

A special provincial committee announced almost similar findings – concentrations of DDT had been found in Ontario fish but studies showed the levels were not yet hazardous to humans.

There is a double irony of sorts in this analysis for the bugs, which no longer have to face agonizing convulsive deaths from DDT.

While countless species were becoming immune to DDT and its derivatives (Aldrin, Dieldrin and Heptachlore), the gummy white powder was considered the best in its field. It was cheap, and its persistence contributed to its low cost as well as its efficiency and humans exposed to DDT in a chemical factory during a period of 18 years received no adverse effects.

But what do the restrictions mean? The bugs still face death from dozens of other reliable alternatives to DDT, but who knows what new rip-roaring species will arise after DDT's suppressive powers are removed this summer.

The chemical industry, bleeding freely from the loss of the DDT market, now must face expenditures of millions of dollars on research for replacements, probably few of which will sport the wide benefits of DDT.

Finally, several of the alternatives are much more toxic, like Parathion for example, an insecticide useful in knocking off bugs that attack potted plants. But manufacturers shudder when recommending it, for Parathion is a real killer and its application demands extraordinary caution.

No wonder the bugs are having the last laugh.

DDT, or Dichlorodiphenyltrichloroethane, was originally synthesized by a German chemistry student in 1874 but its insecticidal properties didn't become apparent until 1939. A Swiss chemist, Dr. Paul Mueller, found that when DDT contacted an insect's nerve endings, the bug underwent muscle spasms leading to death.

For his work in locating an insecticide that need not be ingested by the insect, Dr. Mueller received the Nobel Prize in 1948.

"He deserved it," said Prof. Freeman McEwen, a professor of zoology at the University of Guelph, a field entomologist for 20 years and a staunch opponent of the DDT restrictions.

"You talk about wonder drugs. I think you have to put DDT at the top of the list for the role that it has played in world health."

DDT was one of the greatest heroes in the Second World War, combating malaria in the South Pacific. It reduced the incidence of 27 diseases, saving millions of lives and eliminating an estimated 200 million illnesses in humans.

Then the blessing turned to somewhat of a curse. When DDT entered civilian service, it was sprayed on fruit farms to control flies on Michigan's Mackinac Island and traces of it began to appear in milk around 1949.

In Ontario, where in 1968 DDT used to control pests totalled 306,000 pounds, concern grew about large amounts of the chemical appearing in fish. Government tests showed that fish in Lake Simcoe and in the

Muskoka region had so much DDT in their systems that they were incapable of rearing offspring.

In the 1950s, DDT was sprayed to kill elm bark beatles tearing the sustenance from Dutch Elms, and while the beetles began dying, so did great numbers of robins. Researchers discovered that earthworms were eating DDT-covered leaves on the ground and the worms in turn were eaten by the robins which died of nerve poisoning.

That the earthworms lived and the robins died is a demonstration of the phenomenon known as biological magnification – while the DDT level in one area may be microscopically low, it can multiply through the food chain.

Absorbed into the tiny plankton found in every body of natural water, DDT is transferred to small water creatures that feed on plankton to small fish such as Coho salmon that eat these creatures to larger fish which are in turn eaten by even larger fish and by water fowl and animals.

Because DDT accumulates in the body and is not expelled as waste, even the tiniest amounts absorbed by plankton can result in residues of 10, 20 or 30 parts per million in the large fish at the end of the food chain.

In birds such as the Mallard duck and American eagle, DDT causes the liver to produce enzymes that attack the hormones governing calcium production. When an eagle's system produces less calcium, the egg shells become thinner, causing more frequent breakage and fewer baby eagles. Some scientists say it causes cancer.

DDT eventually has found its way to humans through the food chain and now it is estimated that each of us has a daily intake of .04 milligrams and carries eight ppm in our body fat where DDT is stored. The World Health Organization says humans can consume .7 milligrams of DDT per day without apparent harm, 95 per cent more than we are in fact consuming.

The effects have been shown but the causes are more nebulous. In 1967 Muskoka lake trout carried an average of 19.7 ppm while Lake Simcoe trout showed DDT levels of only 12.55 to 18.44 ppm, even though DDT was being used heavily in the Holland Marshes which drain into Lake Simcoe. The DDT, however, usually remained in the Holland Marsh soil and didn't drain off.

The biggest problem, Prof. McEwen said, was really DDT's use on recreational areas. Aircraft sprayed the stuff into marshes to regulate blackflies and mosquitoes and since DDT is almost insoluble it settled on mud and eventually entered the food chain.

The use of DDT for aerial spraying in parks has been banned for several years by the Ontario department of lands and forests. In addition, DDT, Aldrin and Heptachlore, have been used extensively in Ontario for agricultural use.

Dr. C. R. Harris, head of the soil-pesticide division of the federal department of agriculture in London, Ont., said soils in many agricultural areas are contaminated with residues of these materials or their breakdown products.

Although agriculture has received the brunt of the attack on pesticides and the DDT restrictions, in most cases the degree of soil contamination is not great, Dr. Harris said.

"The evidence is that at the levels of pesticides present in Ontario soils our crops are not picking up significant residues. Our food grown on these soils present no hazard for human consumption," added Prof. McEwen.

What about the urban dweller who buys five pounds of DDT, dusts his rose bushes, then decides to water them, flushing the chemical down the nearest storm sewer and into a receiving stream?

"If you take a hard look at the statistics, about 70 to 75 per cent of all pesticides are used in agriculture. The rest of it is used for recreational purposes and around the home," Prof. McEwen said.

Homeowners find they have a bottle of pesticide hanging around from summer, so to keep it from the kids they indiscriminately dump it down the sink or use extremely heavy applications and it finds its way to Lake Erie, Prof. McEwen said.

"To my knowledge, no one has done a research study on how much of our pollution problem is due to this kind of foolishness in handling pesticides," he said.

Restrictions were needed but the federal and provincial government went much too far, Prof. McEwen believes. Caught in a cost-price squeeze farmers willingly obeyed instructions on DDT container labels and applied only what they felt necessary to remain competitive.

"When you get into the volume farmers use, you follow the regulations because you can't afford to put on twice as much as needed. It wouldn't do a better job. All it does is double your spray bill."

In Prof. McEwen's judgment, the deaths of birds and fish are direct results of DDT's misuse in recreational and urban fields. "I would put prohibitions on home-owners and campers and any users where DDT was likely to get into our water supplies."

His stand is supported by Dr. Harris, who this week said people of Ontario and Canada have been given a "snow job" and advocated sale of pesticides by prescription, much the same as drugs.

DDT was being phased out even before the restrictions were imposed, primarily because insects were becoming more immune to it, the chemical was leaking into lakes and rivers, and foods began to contain a residue arbitrarily in excess of one ppm. The former acceptable level was seven ppm but the federal government has reduced the permissible level in common vegetables and fruits to one ppm.

It is difficult to say just how much DDT was being used as a political lever, but the World Health Organization and Food and Agricultural Organization of the United Nations are attempting to establish an international food code which will set tolerances for all international food shipments.

What the Canadian and Ontario restrictions did was to hasten the process of finding alternatives to DDT, and Aldrin, Dieldrin and Heptachlore which were banned earlier last year.

Complete alternatives to pesticides are possible but none have advanced to a level for grower use. They include:

– Parasites and predators: beneficial insects released to feed on harmful insects.

– Insect diseases: several of hundreds of insect diseases are now under study.

– Plant resistance to insects: some varieties of corn have become resistant to the European corn borer.

– Sterilization techniques: designed to produce insect sterility by radiation or chemical use.

– Hormones: used repeatedly, they would hopefully upset the insect's life cycle normally synchronized with seasons or a host plant.

– Sex attractants: "pheromones," or chemicals released by the male or female to attract the opposite sex for mating can be used as baits to attract either sex to a bait pail for killing.

There are others but few are available except in specific instances. DDT, unfortunately, has only one major alternative, other pesticides, and Prof. McEwen can list more than 50. None have that blanket effect produced by DDT, however. But most are effective killers.

One insecticide that has already been earmarked for a DDT alternative is Diazinon whose role caused all the furor on Ward Island in Toronto about a reputed duck kill. It is especially effective in fly control.

"But I don't know of any of the alternatives that wouldn't cost at least four times as much to do the job."

Recommendations for use of chemicals on various crops were made by government, university and industrial personnel last fall and will be made available shortly.

The cost factor remains one of the big reasons that the World Health Organization cannot afford to move from DDT despite the political factor. DDT's biggest use is in WHO programs and that has not been significantly curtailed. At present WHO says it has no suitable substitute for DDT.

The increase in food prices to the consumer will not be sharp and Prof. McEwen knows of no crop that will be put out of production by the DDT restriction.

"Many of these people don't recognize the fact that pesticides are necessary. For the past 25 years there have been no wormy vegetables on the market," Prof. McEwen said.

"People under 40 have never been exposed to pest-ridden produce. You have a whole generation which doesn't realize pests are a problem. If you remove all uses of pesticides you could no longer produce many of our fruits and vegetables in Ontario. You couldn't produce one apple that wasn't wormy."

"But you come down to the question 'will the alternatives be safer?' and the answer is 'no'," Prof. McEwen warned.

An insecticide's toxicity is measured by its LD50, or the dosage at which half the population exposed to the chemical would die. DDT's LD50 is 115, and that means if 50 persons swallowed 115 milligrams of DDT per kilogram of body weight, 25 of them would be expected to die.

In other words, an average person would have to consume ¼-ounce of actual DDT to get a 50 per cent likelihood of poisoning.

For comparison, highly toxic Parathion's LD50 is eight; Methoxychlor's is 6,000, but although it belongs to the same family as DDT it costs three or four times as much and is much less effective.

DDT can be handled without apparent danger because its lethal dosage through skin absorption is a high 2,500 milligrams per kilogram of body weight, and this explains why persons during the Second World War could open their shirts and dust themselves down for fleas and lice without committing suicide.

Formulators of DDT in Canada expect to be hit hard by the restrictions. There are about 50 companies in Canada's pesticides industry but only three actually produce basic pesticide chemicals.

Nearly all the major firms are subsidiaries of U.S. firms and merely formulate products with imported ingredients. Formulating means mixing with talc to form a dust or with a liquid solvent to form a spray.

Prof. McEwen estimates the value of the annual at-the-factory North American production of DDT at about $20 million, or 140 million pounds at 16 or 17 cents a pound. But he adds that, although the amount seems small, producers fear their return on investment in new products will be discouraging.

"The attitude is critical because it costs about $5 million from the time a chemical is synthesized on the shelf until the first pound is sold," he said. "In other words there is a $5 million research investment in a new pesticide before any return.

"With the public attitude against pesticides, shareholders are getting hesitant to invest this kind of money, especially since agricultural chemicals in general have been low returners. And it takes about five or six years at a minimum for proper research."

Lloyd Miller, manager of the agricultural chemicals division at Shell Canada Ltd. and a director of the Canadian Agricultural Chemical Association, believes the DDT controversy never should have entered the political arena.

"I can't understand what the hell has got into people's minds," he said. "You can swim in DDT. It's true it does stay in the soil a long time but we really don't know what side effects some of these others might have.

"You can't take these products off the market and not get hurt. Certainly we're hurt. We bleed pretty red on this."

Shell has other compounds to replace DDT, he said, so it's just a question of other products doing the same job but not as well and not as cheaply.

A. D. St. Clair, general manager of Diamond Alkali Canada Ltd., estimates that about 800 tons of 100 per cent DDT (before formulation) were sold into the trade last year. Of this, about 600 tons were used in agriculture and household areas, and the remainder in municipal spraying programs. In Canada the annual average use of DDT is less than ½ pound per person.

Of the 800 tons, probably about 60 per cent came to Ontario. "Chances are that the amount of DDT used this year will be about 25 per cent of what was used last year," Mr. St. Clair said. "I'm not expecting to make any money on DDT this year."

Agricultural dealers who normally sell their entire volume to the tobacco industry and other legal users are home free, but the real pinch will be felt by the dealer who offers small packages of DDT to homeowners, Mr. St. Clair said. About $250,000 worth of DDT is now on the shelves of dealers and jobbers in Canada.

The government's near-ban removes DDT from places where it still can be safely used, maintains Byron Beeler, director of the department of agriculture and food's soils and crops branch.

Research at the Canada department of agriculture's research station at Vineland Station shows Niagara Peninsula grape growers should still use DDT, and it could still be used for subterranean cutworms in tomato, pepper and eggplant crops, but not around water, Mr. Beeler said.

"It probably should be made available for the 1970 crop season. Hopefully we would have a replacement for 1971 for this species of cutworm," he said.

Now grape growers must resort to Sevin or Carbaryl which are two to three times as expensive as DDT.

Despite the fear of DDT's effects on soil, like most other dead matter it will receive a burial. Collections are being handled by individual municipalities and local public health units under the guidance of the Ontario department of health.

Its disposal remains in the hands of the waste management branch of the department of energy and resources management and Wes Williamson, a senior waste management engineer in Toronto, said DDT will be buried in suitable landfill sites free from surface or ground water.

It is yet impossible to estimate the amount of DDT and other restricted pesticides that must be buried but in the Niagara Peninsula alone about 360 gallons of liquid spray and 1,060 pounds of powder have been collected. Figures are not available for Hamilton or Wentworth County.

In Toronto, seven tons of pesticides have been collected and three tons each in St. Thomas and Thunder Bay.

But there are still rumbles of dissent. "The safest way to dispose of the present DDT stock now is to use it," Mr. St. Clair maintained. Prof. McEwen advocates a pesticide control board composed of authorities in the field to ensure strict supervision of chemicals and communication of reasoned arguments to the province, not emotional appeals.

# Mysterious Pollution:
# The Green Infection

## P. T. Boylan

LONDON – A detailed report has been published in a British journal by the team of biologists who investigated the mysterious green infection that nearly destroyed the 16,000-year-old cave paintings of Lascaux, in France. Their findings are important because they indicate how human interference can cause irreparable damage to cave sites unless there is careful control.

The report by Marcel Lefevre and Guy Laporte, of the French Hydrobiological Research Centre, describes how contaminating material on the shoes of visitors and an alarming change in the growth pattern of a species of algae nearly destroyed unique evidence of the artistic sense of Upper Paleolithic man.

It is published in the international journal *Studies in Speleology*, produced by the William Pengelly Cave Studies Trust, Devon. The cause of the green growth was the spread of the algae, in complete darkness, as they multiplied on humanly introduced organic debris such as sweat and bacteria. The treatment devised to combat the infection had severe side effects.

The Lascaux paintings were discovered in 1940 and declared an historic monument. After the war the caves were opened for an enormous number of visitors. In September, 1960, a patch of green mold was noticed on the wall of the Hall of the Bulls.

The patch grew rapidly and further patches were seen to be developing in many other places and obscuring the paintings. A French Government scientific commission was set up to investigate the "malade verte" and the cave was closed.

The report by Lefevre and Laporte indicates that the paintings at Lascaux are now safe, but several disquieting facts emerge – not least the sudden change in growth pattern of one of the species of algae after 20 years of apparent stability, the serious effect of the treatment used on the harmless occupants of the cave, and the obvious threat of a similar disaster elsewhere if large numbers of visitors are allowed into such important caves.

*Intensive Study*

The biologists began by making a detailed study in the field and in the laboratory of the infected areas and found a considerable microfauna and flora. However, only one element was undergoing the huge multiplication to produce the visible contamination of the paintings – a species of the green alga Palmellococcus.

This is common in the soil and on wet rocks in the vicinity of the cave itself and is attributed to a combination of factors: the enlargement of the original opening of the cave to admit visitors, the use of unpurified water in the air-conditioning system and, above all, the introduction of soil and slime on the feet of visitors.

The spread of the infection was attributed to the rapid circulation of air by an overworked air-conditioning plant, and it was believed that the algal growths were encouraged by the artificial lighting in the cave. The lights and air-conditioning were turned off and for three months the cave was virtually sealed. After this period detailed examination showed that the number of infected sites had increased 10 times when normal alga growths should have almost ceased.

The research team argues convincingly that this alarming development, and the sudden flare-up of the trouble so long after the opening of the cave, was due to a fundamental change in the growth pattern of Palmellococcus from the normal light-dependent condition to a rarer "heterothrophic" pattern in which the plant effectively uses organic substances – such as the sweat, pollen and bacteria brought in by visitors – as a substitute for light in the growth process.

*Risk to Paintings*

After laboratory studies a treatment was devised for spraying the infected areas with a dilute solution of formaldehyde. It killed the algae and bleached the dead cells which were left on the wall, but could not be removed because of the risk of damaging the fragile painted surfaces.

Before treatment the cave was fumigated with aerosol dispersions of broad-spectrum antibiotics – penicillin, streptomycin and kanamycin – to disperse humanly introduced bacteria. After the walls of the cave had been sprayed the entrance and the cave floor were treated with a strong solution of formaldehyde with detergent – a process that is now repeated regularly.

Within three months it was obvious that the treatment had been successful, apart from one minor regrowth three years later. Lascaux cave is still closed to the public and may remain so unless the visitor can be completely separated from the paintings. But it is possible for scientists to visit the cave under strictly controlled conditions.

Discussion of the near-disaster at Lascaux goes beyond the question of methods of killing algal growths on irreplaceable art treasures. The number of visitors has already seriously damaged the cave through organic contamination of the atmosphere and the cave floor. But the treatment used, together with the continued use of disinfectants in the entrance area, must have irreparably destroyed the natural environment of the cave.

The main lesson is that the cave environment is a rare and extremely delicate one. There is always a great risk in opening up any cave of scientific importance, whether for tourists or for sporting cavers. The risk of contamination of an important scientific site is so great that no new cave system should ever be opened up until there has been a thorough scientific investigation leading to a definite management plan, which might involve a drastic restriction on access to avoid damage to an important environment.

# Part E

# Man the Waste-Maker

*Canadians are part of the "throw-away" society. Non-return bottles, disposable diapers, cans, and fancy packaging all add to the creation of waste. It is estimated that one-half of the groceries purchased by a housewife each week is removed from the household as garbage. Canadians enjoy a high standard of living, and account for some 1,800 pounds of waste per person annually. Disposing of this waste creates an enormous problem, especially in large cities.*

*Both Canada and the United States face similar problems of waste disposal. Abrahams, in his article,* Wealth Out of Waste, *outlines the difficulties that waste disposal creates in the United States. He also suggests some logical, but unusual solutions. For municipal and industrial wastes, new techniques are being developed, such as the Cantraco process for sewage treatment.*

# A New and Cheap Way
# of Treating Wastes

MONTREAL – A Montreal company says it has developed a revolutionary method of treating municipal and industrial wastes.

The new system uses oxygen and ozone to remove up to 99% of micro-organisms and certain poisons from waste material. It was developed by Canatraco Ltd., which manufactures ozone-producing equipment.

Recently field tests were carried out on municipal waste, principally sewage, in Granby, Que. The city's director of technical services, M. Andre Laliberte, says the results were excellent. Coliform counts were reduced by nearly 100% after treatment with the Canatraco process.

The company's principal innovation is to treat the waste material as it passes through disposal pipes, rather than in holding tanks at the outlet of the pipe. Mr. Karel Stopka, president of Canatraco, says the elimination of holding tanks and other peripheral equipment cuts the cost of sewage treatment by as much as 70%.

The Canatraco process injects oxygen into the sewage, cultivating the micro-organisms which are present, and then applies ozone under hydraulic pressure. Mr. Stopka says all micro-organisms can be killed in less than 15 minutes. Offensive odors and colors are removed.

Since ozone is an isotope which will revert rapidly to oxygen, it does not create unwanted side-effects.

Research and development for the process have been carried out over the past seven years, and have cost more than $100,000. The next step will probably be a demonstration plant for municipal sewage treatment, capable of handling 5 million gallons of raw sewage a day. The company is negotiating with Central Mortgage and Housing Corp. for financial assistance in building the plant.

At its current stage of development, the process involves only primary treatment of sewage. But further development will involve secondary and tertiary treatment as well.

A number of cities in Europe and the U.S. use ozone in water purification plants rather than the conventional chlorination process. Canatraco has had two invitations to install its equipment in the U.S. and is considering licensing an American manufacturer.

Municipal waste treatment is an almost untouched market. The high cost of conventional waste treatment has prevented many cities from installing treatment plants. Canatraco says that its process is cheap enough to be bought by even very small municipalities.

Ozone can also be used to treat industrial wastes containing cyanide and phenol, which are by-products of many industrial processes. The process oxidizes the poisonous materials and renders them harmless.

Tests on Canatraco equipment by Falconbridge Nickel Mines Ltd. have shown an 85% reduction in the poisonous content of waste water. Falconbridge says more work is needed to judge the economic feasibility of the process for industrial use, however.

Canatraco has demonstrated its process to federal government officials and has applied for grants under Ottawa's incentive programs for industrial research, development and innovation.

# Wealth Out of Waste

## John H. Abrahams, Jr.

An international survey of 12 countries conducted by America's leading anti-litter organization, Keep America Beautiful, Inc., finds a strong correlation between a nation's standard of living and the amount of trash it produces. In India, for example, the equivalent of 200 pounds of refuse per capita is discarded each year. But in the affluent United States we annually average some 1,800 pounds of waste for each individual.

That's a lot of waste, yet only about 10 per cent of it consists of what most people think of as "real garbage," food scraps and the like. Some 90 per cent is rubbish – cans, papers, bottles, junky appliances, bald tires, rickety furniture and so forth, as shown in Table I.

TABLE I

## COMPOSITION OF REPRESENTATIVE MUNICIPAL WASTE

| ITEM | PER CENT BY WEIGHT |
|---|---|
| Corrugated paper boxes | 25.70 |
| Newspapers | 10.34 |
| Magazine paper | 7.47 |
| Brown paper | 6.13 |
| Mail | 3.02 |
| Paper food cartons | 2.27 |
| Tissue paper | 2.18 |
| Plastic coated paper and wax paper | 1.68 |
| Subtotal | 58.79 |
| Vegetable and fruit wastes | 4.20 |
| Meat scraps (cooked) and fried fats | 5.04 |
| Subtotal | 9.24 |
| Wood | 2.52 |
| Ripe tree leaves, flower garden plants, evergreens, and lawn grass (green) | 7.56 |
| Subtotal | 10.08 |
| Metal | 7.52 |
| Glass, ceramics, ash | 8.49 |
| Miscellaneous: Plastics, rags, leather and rubber goods, paints and oils, parts, and dirt | 5.88 |
| | 100.00 |

Composited from typical compositions for research purposes. Adapted from Remson, Irwin; A. Alexander Fungaroli, and Alonzo W. Lawrence, *Water Movement in an Unsaturated Sanitary Landfill*. Journal of the Sanitary Engineering Division, Proceedings of the American Society of Civil Engineers, Vol. 94, SA 2, April 1968.

It goes without saying that the bigger the city the bigger the problem. A community of 60,000 might produce some 30,000 tons of residential

refuse annually. New York City produces three times that much every week. The city, 13 per cent of which used to be dumping grounds, is custodian of the world's largest dump. Three hundred men are assigned to a 2,800-acre landfill on Staten Island in shifts that work 24 hours a day unloading 600-ton barges that shuttle back and forth from Lower Manhattan. Officially the city estimates it has eight years worth of landfill remaining. Unofficially the word is four years. Whichever, the fact remains that nobody has presented a valid plan for what to do next.

*Unacceptable Situation*

New York isn't unique, just big. Most municipalities still dispose of their solid wastes by some land disposal method, more often than not an ordinary open dump. Unfortunately, the U.S. Public Health Service reports that more than 90 per cent of these dumps – there are some 12,000 throughout the nation – are "unacceptable and represent disease potential, threat of pollution, and land blight."

What about the 300-odd municipal incinerators that exist today? The record is only slightly better. Public Health experts say about 75 per cent are inadequate. Generally they are inefficient, not burning enough of the materials dumped into them and becoming contributors to local air pollution problems.

And so, we find ourselves at a crossroads. We can continue on our present course of burn and bury – and eventual chaos – or we can start planning now for a balanced "systems" approach to salvage and reuse. Solid waste management is, after all, more of a materials handling problem than a health problem.

At present we are letting a tremendous lot of our waste go to waste. Our natural resources aren't as limitless as we once thought and much of what we call "waste" actually comprises potential renewable resources. Industry, because of its intimate knowledge of its own products and the materials from which they are made, can make vital contributions toward solution of solid waste problems. Through the combined efforts of industry and government, new technology is being developed to accomplish two basic goals: reduction in the volume of solid wastes as soon after discarding as possible and productive use of all salvageable materials.

## Incinerators Leave Rich Ore

High temperature incineration at about 2,500°F. produces the greatest reduction in volume, approximately 95 per cent, with some possible use of excess heat and of the remaining slag. However, regular incineration and a burning process called pyrolysis seem to offer better opportunities for salvage.

The U.S. Bureau of Mines reports that residues from refuse incinerators are as much as 30 per cent metal and 45 per cent glass, which is rich ore. The bureau has awarded a special grant to the American Public Works Association to conduct in-depth studies of six cities in an effort to determine the best and most economical ways of recycling such salvageable materials. The cities are Baltimore, Cincinnati, Milwaukee, Atlanta, New Orleans, and Los Angeles.

Bureau of Mines experts conducted their own studies of incinerator operations near Washington, D.C., Atlanta, and New Orleans and estimated that the cost of separating the metal and glass in a ton of residue, utilizing a plant capable of processing 250 tons a day, would be about $3.50. The cost includes an expensive hand picking step to remove massive iron fragments. However, a continuous, fully automated system is being developed by the bureau and is expected to lower the cost considerably. And after this processing it no longer will be a problem of solid wastes, but rather one of refining constituent materials.

In South Pasadena, Calif., the Stanford Research Institute has contracts with the U.S. Public Health Service's Bureau of Solid Waste

TABLE II

CURRENT VALUE RANGES OF
SEPARATED WASTE FRACTIONS

| | |
|---|---|
| Composted waste (organic) | $4 to $12 per ton |
| Ferrous metals | $20 to $40 per ton |
| Non-ferrous metals (copper, lead, zinc, tin) | Approximately $5.00 per ton of rubbish |
| Aluminum | $50.00 to $100.00 per ton of separated scrap |
| Glass | $6 to $12 per ton ($6 for mixed cullet; $12 for clean cullet) |

Compiled 1969 by Naturizer Corporation, Norman, Okla.

Management and the Glass Container Manufacturers Institute to conduct experiments on separation of raw refuse for salvage purposes. Using what it calls a modified air classification system, the institute estimates a cost as low as 10 cents a ton for a critical separation of refuse, including operating costs and amortization of equipment. Grinding or shredding of refuse before separation is estimated at an additional 40 to 60 cents a ton.

*Is Salvage Economically Feasible?*

Naturizer Corp. of Norman, Okla., a firm applying a total environmental systems approach to waste management, reports that separation and resale of municipal waste materials is economically feasible now. The company points out that resale values of various separated waste components are difficult to establish because only small quantities of such separated materials are currently available for market analysis. However, it has compiled some value ranges, subject to market and transportation considerations, from current information, as shown in Table II. Other by-products of solid wastes are being developed, according to Naturizer, such as animal feed from composted municipal refuse and organic gases and charcoal from pyrolysis processes. Both show promise of profitability as well as providing additional outlets for waste products, although no economic breakdowns are available yet.

The goal of most industry-sponsored research in the solid waste field is to make large-scale salvage of materials economically feasible. The aluminum industry in 1967 salvaged and recycled 1.7 billion pounds of aluminum scrap, about 20 per cent of that year's total supply, while the ferrous scrap industry in 1968 salvaged 4.5 million tons for remelting by steel mills and foundries. The American Paper Institute reports that nearly one-fifth of its industry's annual production also is recycled.

In my own area, the Glass Container Manufacturers Institute, Inc., represents more than 90 per cent of the nation's glass producing capacity. GCMI started an extensive study of the solid waste situation shortly after passage of the Solid Waste Disposal Act of 1965. Programs including study of air and water pollution were begun, but the main thrust was development of improved methods of disposing of solid wastes, with special emphasis on glass containers and other packaging materials. According to a recent survey, glass was found to account for approximately 6 per cent of U.S. refuse and between 1 and 15 per cent in other countries.

GCMI's solid waste program has three main objectives. First is salvage and reuse of glass in the glass making process. Quality control and cost considerations make this more complex than it might appear. The second objective is development of secondary uses for glass; for instance: in the manufacture of decorations, specialty paints, insulation, and building materials. Again, quality control is a major consideration and the market now for reused glass in these areas is minor. Further development is essential. The third objective of GCMI's solid waste program is to facilitate inclusion of glass in normal waste disposal processes.

## Waste Glass in Asphalt

A number of interesting potential uses for waste glass currently are being explored. The University of Missouri at Rolla, for instance, is demonstrating the feasibility of using crushed waste glass as the aggregate in asphalt. Scientists there found that the amount of glass disposed of in many municipalities was about the same as the amount of limestone used in asphalt for street patching projects. They estimated that the cost of preparing the waste glass for reuse would be no more than the cost of the limestone it would replace, plus the present disposal costs of waste glass.

A test patch of the glass-asphalt mixture has been in place in a university parking lot for more than a year. It has withstood heavy traffic

*Glass-asphalt paving, Scarborough, Ontario.*

under all weather conditions and shows no evidence of unusual wear, according to the researchers. In all respects, they report, its serviceability is comparable to a normal asphalt concrete. The study is continuing under a research grant awarded by the Bureau of Solid Waste Management.

Ceramic specialists of the Bureau of Mines' research center at Tuscaloosa, Ala., are developing several novel methods of using the glass portion of either incinerator residue or raw refuse. They have made a variety of extremely attractive bricks by bonding glass with different types of industrial materials, such as aluminum phosphate, sodium silicate, slaked lime, and even phosphate slimes. The bricks are said to meet official specifications for "severe weathering bricks" without difficulty.

The same group of researchers also is working on methods of transforming melted waste glass into a kind of "wool" that would be suitable for use as insulating material. In addition, they have created samples of a very light, strong honeycomb-like glass material that shows promise as a lightweight aggregate suitable for construction purposes.

*Waste Could Be a Utility*

However, before experimental solutions to most municipal disposal problems can hope to succeed, a great deal of progress must be made in the disposal system itself. Mechanization and automation must be increased substantially if salvage and recycling are to become economically feasible. At present, the "industry" of residential solid waste collection is among the last to give up hand methods. Development of bigger, more powerful compactor equipment is about the extent of progress.

Eventually, I believe management of solid wastes is going to have to be considered rather like a utility, to be handled with the same type of strict organization and regulation that today is typical of light, power, and gas utilities. The scope of burgeoning waste problems certainly warrants such attention.

My own idea of an ideal waste disposal system for a community is based on two premises: first, that the ultimate solution lies in a combination rather than a single approach to the problem; second, that salvage, reuse and recycling are fundamental to a successful solution.

Obviously the closer to the consumer that a salvage operation can start, the more efficient it will be. Ideally glass, metal, paper and other such materials would be segregated initially in homes, hotels, shopping centers, and the other establishments that are major waste producers. Of course, resistance to such on-the-spot salvage schemes has been great. If it remains so, there should then be a system of regional distribution stations to which wastes would be transported by conventional garbage trucks until other means of transfer are developed.

These stations would be designed to separate the refuse instead of compacting or baling it as is done today. Paper, rags and similar material would be separated, baled and shipped to appropriate mills for reuse. The glass would be returned to manufacturers, and the scrap metals would be sent to the melting furnaces of steel mills, foundries, and refineries to help make new products. Garbage and vegetable waste material would be composted.

Systems of this type are being developed now and several pilot plants are operating and soon should be ready for field testing. For additional benefits, sludge and agricultural wastes could be mixed with the compost to increase its fertilizer value and possibly be spread on public lands.

In other words, everything would be used and used again, leaving only a small fraction of material to actually be "thrown away" – and much of that being returned to the land in some beneficial manner.

A scientific report submitted to the Senate Public Works Committee in 1968 put the situation rather succinctly when it stated:

"It is now evident that the industrial economy of the United States must undergo a shift from a use and discard approach to a closed cycle of use and salvage, reprocess, and reuse . . . or else face the alternative of a congested planet that has turned into a polluted trash heap."

# Part F

# The Deafening Din

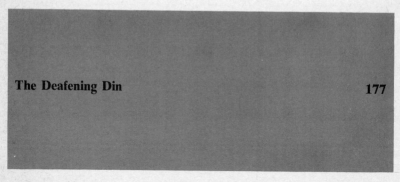

*Although noise has not been emphasized as an environmental problem in Canada yet, there are evidences that it cannot be ignored much longer. Near Vancouver airport, a public school has been specially insulated to enable classes to continue while jet planes fly overhead. Planners in Ontario are experimenting with special noise screens to protect residential areas adjacent to Highway 401 in Metropolitan Toronto, but these are only tiny indications of the concern that should develop. It is hoped that the accompanying article,* The Deafening Din, *will help to awaken Canadians to the problem.*

# The Deafening Din

*Preface*

*Up to now many of the dangerous and hazardous effects of intense noise on human health have been seriously underestimated. Yet recent forecasts suggest that if city noise continues to rise at the present rate of one decibel a year, we all could be stone deaf by the year 2000. This issue of* The Balance *takes a look at the growing problem of noise pollution.*

Although Americans now are concerned about air and water pollution problems, most of us have overlooked one of the most pervasive and potentially destructive forms of disturbance – noise. Noise, like air and water pollution, can damage our health, lower the quality of our living environment and lessen our enjoyment of leisure time activities.

A person's response to sound (defined as any sensation perceived by the sense of hearing) is affected not only by loudness, pitch and duration, but also by the hearer's own physical and mental state. Thus the sound of a sports car revving up, of an elk bugling, rock music, a train whistle or the roar of a waterfall, though all relatively high in decibels, can be enjoyable and stimulating, depending on how tuned-in you are. Noise, on the other hand, is defined as "a sound that lacks agreeable musical quality or is noticeably loud, harsh, or discordant." It is dangerous when it is loud, irregular and unexpected as in a sonic boom or the sudden roar of a motorcycle.

Modern noise is insidious because we have become so accustomed to it in our everyday lives that we no longer seem to mind, or possibly even notice it. In effect, people have increased their reaction threshold.

*From Sea to Shining Sea*, the report of the President's Council on Recreation and Natural Beauty, states:

> Sounds are an integral part of urban life. The parade, the concert
> in the park, the street peddlers, the clanging of the cable car,
> all belong to the exciting history of the city. Sounds have intensi-
> fied in this industrial age to a point where they now constitute
> a form of pollution of the environment.

Some say that consumers have become so used to a certain level of noise that they demand it. For example, a housewife may not believe her vacuum cleaner is doing the job unless she hears "the sound of power." But this attitude may not continue. In 1968 the Evinrude Company produced its first quiet-model outboard motor which in one year outsold all its noisy competitors combined.

Public concern is increasing as more people are becoming aware of the fact that an untold number of men, women, and children are suffering disabilities resulting from noise. Introducing a report prepared by the Office for Science and Technology, former President Lyndon Johnson commented, "A minimum of 6,000,000 and perhaps as many as 16,000,000 industrial workers are threatened with degrees of loss of hearing from exposure to noise on the job." He also noted that overall sound levels have been doubling every 10 years.

## The Measurement of Noise

The decibel is the unit used to measure sound. The smallest sound an acute human ear can perceive in quiet surroundings is about one decibel. Three decibels represents the smallest difference that the human ear can ordinarily detect between the loudness of two sounds. An increase of three decibels means the intensity of the sound source or amplifier has doubled. However, an increase of nine decibels is necessary before the sound is perceptively doubled. Decibels increase logarithmically

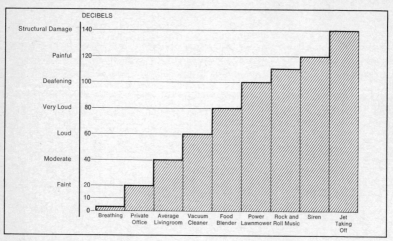

Figure 1. *Typical Sound Pressure Levels.*

rather than arithmetically, so for each additional .10 decibels sound intensity is multiplied by 10.

Man's annoyance threshold for intermittent sounds, according to the Conservation Foundation, is from 50 to 90 decibels, while the pain threshold is 120. Anything above 80 decibels is likely to be uncomfortable. At 90 or above, the experts begin worrying about the effects on health.

One common household appliance, the food blender, emits 93 decibels, and a subway train screeching around a curved track reaches 95. The motorcyclist revving up his bike generates about 110, and a jet plane taking off will assault unprotected ears with 150. Some other decibel levels of everyday noise-makers include: garbage disposal units, 80; riveting guns, 110; busy rush-hour traffic, 85; and power lawnmowers, 95.

## Noise, Noise Everywhere

Scientists and legislators both are becoming concerned about the growing clamor in our work environment, our homes, and even in our recreation areas. Senator Gordon Allott of Colorado, in a recent statement on environmental problems, made the point that the noise level of our cities has been increasing at the rate of one decibel per year. "If this continued," Allott said, "all city inhabitants would be deaf by the year 2000."

Already when urban man travels to work, whether in his private car or by public transportation, he is traveling in a vehicle that exposes him to dangerously high noise levels. Once at the office he is plagued by a cacophony of typewriters, calculators and other business machines. One New York bank suffered such employee turnover in its noisy check tabulating room that it resorted to hiring deaf people.

Noise pollution is not restricted to the factory and the big city. Dance halls, the kitchen, or even the lawn of a surburban home on a Sunday afternoon can become painfully noisy places. Suburban man is besieged by the sounds of television sets, garbage disposals, clanging garbage cans, lawnmowers and the like. He is forced to listen not only to his excessively noisy appliances, but those of his neighbors as well. Many discotheques and teen-age school dances produce sound levels above 110 decibels which cannot be endured for more than a few minutes without damage to the ears.

Noise in and around our homes and apartments is so bad that many city people depend on an air-conditioner to blanket exterior noises. In cold weather when an air-conditioner isn't needed, people may purchase a little machine called "Sleep-Mate" to simulate the drone of an air-conditioner. Or one may buy a device called "Sleep Sound" which will hum like a breeze in the trees. It is easy to see why city dwellers sometimes find it difficult to sleep when camping out in the quiet of our parks and forests.

Last January, after three years of study, a Task Force on Noise Control in New York City issued a 55-page report entitled *Toward a Quieter City.* The Task Force found that noise in the city regularly went above safe levels. They recommended that sound interfering with the normal level of human speech – above 52 decibels – should be reduced as soon as possible and the desired limit in wholly residential areas be set at 40 decibels in the daytime and 30 at night.

In the past we could escape the tumult of modern day living by retreating to a neighborhood park or forest area. But noise is an increasing problem in our more popular recreation areas – the city park and even the once-remote wilderness. A record number of visitors are invading our recreation areas and bringing with them the sounds of the city – television sets, transistors to blare forth the latest rock tunes, and nearly all the other modern-day conveniences. In addition, more people have cars, trailers, campers, motorcycles, snowmobiles and outboard motors. At the same time overflights of aircraft, both subsonic and supersonic, disturb the outdoor serenity.

*Effects of Excessive Noise on Man*

Sustained moderately high noise level conditions or a sudden blast such as the sonic boom can affect our physical and mental health in a variety of ways. The following are some of the effects we know about.

*Hearing loss* – Continuous noise above 80 decibels can cause hearing loss, and a sound level of 90 decibels can be tolerated only for short periods. Temporary deafness can be caused by even short exposure to levels of 100 to 125. Beyond 150 decibels, the inner ear can be permanently damaged.

Dr. Samuel Rosen, professor of ear surgery at New York's Mount Sinai School of Medicine, says, "The length of time it takes for the body to return to its normal state after exposure to loud noise is roughly the same as the duration of the noise itself. But if it lasts for hours, recovery may take a good deal longer."

Eighteen million Americans suffer from some degree of hearing loss, often from exposure to noise. An estimated two out of three working males are victims of work connected perceptive deafness, caused by the continuous impact of loud sounds. One of the Army's top hearing specialists, Dr. Jerry L. Northern, estimated that more than half of the 500,000 men who go through basic training each year suffer hearing loss so serious they could be medically ruled out of combat.

*Other physical health effects* – Aside from hearing loss, exposure to noise can increase body tensions which in turn can affect blood pressure and the functions of the heart and nervous system. Noise may cause skin to pale, muscles to tense and blood vessels to constrict. It can also trigger such ailments as stomach ulcers and allergies, and cause a general decrease in efficiency. Reports from overseas have even linked high noise levels in factories with sexual impotency.

*Emotional damage* – Noise alone would not ordinarily unhinge a well-adjusted person. But combined with other stress factors – financial problems, a domestic crisis, fatigue or poor health – it can trigger a strong emotional response. Thus a man shot a 13-year-old boy playing in the street, whose shouting, combined with the clamor of the traffic, was keeping him awake. During the Korean War one form of torture used by the North Koreans on captured GI's was to put upended buckets over their heads and bang on the buckets with a stick. This method weakened their resistance more rapidly than did starvation, cold or the non-stop third degree.

A two-year study in an area near London's Heathrow Airport has shown a significantly higher incidence of mental illness requiring treatment among people most exposed to aircraft racket. The study, reported in a British medical journal, was careful not to label noise as the cause of the illness, but it did suggest that it aggravated existing conditions.

*Sleeplessness* – The Stanford Research Institute says that many people show fatigue from the effort to remain asleep in spite of noise. It has been demonstrated that bursts of sound – even though mild enough (55 decibels) not to wake the sleeper – are recorded by the brain. The nervous system responds just as it does during waking hours, turning a deep, restorative sleep into a less beneficial series of catnaps. The study reports repeated interruptions of sleep can have damaging effects, particularly on aged or sick people.

*Super Sounds*

Last September approval was given to continue the development of an American supersonic airplane, a project begun years before. Congress appropriated $80 million for fiscal year 1970 to start building two flying prototypes which will ultimately cost $4.5 billion, and which will fly at speeds up to 1,800 miles per hour. The federal government's share will be around $1 billion. John Volpe, Secretary of Transportation, said that the supersonic transport (SST) will be banned from flying over populated areas until the sonic boom problem is solved. Some question whether technology can ever really find a solution.

Sonic booms are caused by shock waves trailing behind a plane as it reaches the speed of sound (about 600 miles an hour at high altitude). Besides the deafening explosion-like noise, the booms can produce jarring vibrations on the ground. Dr. William A. Shurcliff, Director of the Citizens' League Against the Sonic Boom, makes some interesting observations on the effects of the SST in *The Sonic Boom Handbook*. Dr. Shurcliff points out that the area struck by the sonic boom is not just confined to the region directly below the airplane, but can be as wide as 25 or 50 miles depending upon the topography. As many as 20 million people could be affected by a single trip of the SST across the country.

The sonic boom may be as hazardous to wildlife as it is to man. Conservationists and naturalists have expressed concern over the long-term effects of supersonic flights. In the Wind River Mountains of Wyoming elk have left range which they normally occupy. Some guides and packers in the area believe they have left because of sonic booms. In Switzerland a herd of prize cattle stampeded over a cliff after being frightened by a sonic boom. It was also reported that in 1966, sonic booms resulted in the death of 2,000 baby mink on a farm in Minnesota. A court held that the airplane owner had to pay for the mink killed. Supersonic flights may have adverse effects on the reproduction of fish, and may have a damaging effect on colonies of birds that nest on cliffs.

The fear is that over a long period of time sonic booms may cause the extinction of valuable species of animals.

Sonic booms have reportedly also caused significant damage in many unique natural areas. At Canyon de Muerto National Monument in Arizona, an ancient Indian dwelling was demolished when a large portion of an overhanging cliff fell following a supersonic flight. A rockfall of 66,000 tons occurred at Mesa Verde National Park in Colorado after the passage of two jet planes traveling at speeds greater than sound. In Death Valley Monument (California and Nevada), 323 sonic booms were counted in a six-month period ending in February 1968, with 68 of these considered to be serious enough to cause weakening and demolition of geologic features.

*Things That Can Be Done*

There is no question that the effective implementation of present knowledge would make the United States a more tranquil place. Essentially there are four physical methods by which man can cope with noises: (1) surrounding the source with sound-absorbing material; (2) surrounding the people who would be disturbed with sound-absorbing material; (3) installing a sound suppression device between the people and the source; or (4) simply reducing the noise being produced.

Machines can be designed to be relatively silent. It often means just being more careful in choosing materials they are made of. Many new devices to control noise are now on the market, but the public must be willing to pay the additional cost of quieter products. A relatively noiseless lawnmower costs $15 more than the high-whining models. Among recent American inventions are a "silent residential quality" attachment for pneumatic drills, steel mesh blankets to muffle dynamite blasting, a quiet pile driver, and a portable ground muffler for jet planes to reduce sound during warm-up periods. The din of traffic can be reduced with the improved mufflers now available for all vehicles, including trucks and motorcycles. Plastic pipes for domestic plumbing are quieter and cheaper, but not all local building codes permit them. New materials have also been developed to make quieter road surfaces, and there are quieter tires. Car manufacturers are rising to the challenge by making and advertising quieter cars. The National Aeronautics and Space Administration is doing research on methods of reducing the roar of the jet engine.

Today's noise-jaded homeowner can insist on the use of sound-reducing home construction materials and methods such as double walls, sidewall insulation, staggered studs, sound absorbent ceilings, and tile or pipe-wrapping. According to Dr. Knudsen, spending 5 per cent to 10 per cent more on construction costs can effectively soundproof buildings and reduce noise by as much as 50 decibels. Planting more grass and trees may help also. Research conducted at Riverbank Acoustical Laboratories in Geneva, Illinois, revealed that grass is a highly efficient absorber of sound.

Studies indicate that industrial racket is by far the most important single cause of hearing loss. To alleviate this problem many industries construct buildings and equipment with noise suppression in mind. To help reduce harmful noise in plants with government contracts, new Labor Department regulations set limits ranging from 90 decibels for workers exposed eight hours a day to 115 decibels for exposure of 15 minutes or less per day.

## Regulations and Legislation

The United States lags behind many other nations which long ago recognized noise as an environmental pollutant and adopted national laws to deal with it. Noise regulating laws are in effect in England, France, Germany, and the Scandinavian countries. In some countries transistor radios are banned in public places, vehicles have been silenced and even model airplanes have mufflers. In Sweden, the State Power Board's one-year course in pollution control trains engineers to deal with water, air and noise pollution. Both Sweden and Canada have passed legislation or ordinances against sonic booms. The French confiscate cars ticketed for repeated noise violations. In Switzerland it is an offense to slam a car door too loudly. Moscow bans needless horn-blowing, and several German towns close roads to motor traffic at night.

International concern over excessive sound, particularly sonic boom problems, was indicated by the May 1968 International Congress for Noise Abatement. Delegates from 25 nations adopted a resolution urging their governments to prohibit supersonic flights.

Awareness is also growing in the United States that we have reached a point where concerted efforts are needed to cope with the din around us. The following incident is one reason why official Washington is as involved as it is in trying to curb excessive noise:

Not long after he died in 1967, poet Carl Sandburg was honored at a ceremony at the Lincoln Memorial.

President Johnson sat there while one dignitary after another rose to speak. Johnson couldn't hear much of what they said. Almost all he could hear was the jets overhead, coming down the Potomac on their landing run to National Airport. As his own turn to speak approached, Johnson turned to Interior Secretary Stewart Udall.

"Get rid of those jets," he ordered. A startled Udall spoke to the nearest Secret Service man, who quickly telephoned the presidential command to the airport. By the time Johnson rose to speak the noise had stopped. And throughout his address, the jets remained miles upriver, circling.*

During 1968 the President directed all federal agencies to take account of noise factors in locating and designing buildings, highways, and other projects aided by federal funds. Noise-prevention standards are required by the Department of Housing and Urban Development (HUD) as a condition for certain federal grants. HUD recently hired acoustical consultants to determine whether "added sound" can be used in homes, churches, schools, and hospitals to reduce the impact of aircraft noise. It also is helping finance four studies to come up with ideas for abating aircraft noise in airport areas. A study conducted for the Department of Health, Education and Welfare in 1967, entitled *A Strategy for a Livable Environment*, recommends establishment of tolerance measures and criteria for urban noises.

The 90th Congress passed the first federal law dealing with noise pollution, P.L. 90-411. It requires the Federal Aviation Administration (FAA) to establish regulations to control aircraft noise, including booms from supersonic planes. In November of 1969, the Federal Aviation Administration adopted final noise standards for new, non-supersonic aircraft. The new regulations are weaker than those originally proposed, however. Also it was announced that by 1971 the FAA will probably demand that engines on some 2,100 existing commercial jets be muffled to a still unspecified level.

The only federal attempt so far to define acceptable levels of noise deals with industry. That was an amendment to the Walsh-Healy Act establishing a maximum decibel level of 90 as a standard for all contractors doing business with the government. While 90 decibels is not the gentlest on the ears, at least it is a start.

The Noise Control Act of 1970 (H.R. 15473) is one of several proposals before the 91st Congress to combat noise pollution. It would establish a Noise Control Advisory Council within the Department of Health, Education and Welfare and an Office of Noise Control within the Office of the Surgeon General. The new Office would make grants for the purposes of providing programs of noise control and research into the causes and effects of noise.

A key to effective controls, however, is the setting of standards for

* Roberta Horning and James Welsh, "A World in Danger—5; The Day LBJ was almost Speechless," *Washington Evening Star* (January 15, 1970).

permissive noise levels by state and local governments. Thus far states have generally been lax in the matter of reducing noise levels and only 10 have legal limits. Twenty-five more are considering legal limits on noise. But 41 states do regard noise-induced loss of hearing as a compensatory loss under typical workman's compensation laws.

Attempts by cities to reduce urban pandemonium can be traced to 1929 when New York City established a Noise Abatement Commission. Today many local zoning and building ordinances rigidly require specified materials, methods and equipment. A more useful approach than specification codes which require the achievement of low sound levels. Typically, existing municipal noise ordinances covering construction work only restrict hours of operation; rarely do they prescribe maximum allowable noise levels. This is in spite of the fact that silencing equipment is often available.

Many of our present laws and local ordinances are permissive, not well enforced, and fines are apparently too small to be a deterrent. There are exceptions, however. Memphis and Milwaukee both rigidly enforce motor vehicle noise laws. Memphis has won 13 consecutive annual noise abatement awards. Also Santa Barbara, California and Dearborn, Michigan have passed ordinances banning harmful or annoying booms.

*In Conclusion . . .*

Most of our noisy machines can be toned down or tuned out, if we are determined to do so. It will cost money (a price of somewhere between 5 and 10 per cent more on most products) but so, for example, do other pollution control measures such as sewage treatment. Inaction also will continue to cost money. Senator Mark Hatfield (R-Oregon) says the cost of noise to industry – in compensation, lost production, decreased efficiency – is estimated at over $4 billion per year.

Efforts to dampen the din are only beginning to be made. Designers and manufacturers of machines, cars and planes can greatly contribute to this effort; so can architects, engineers and planners who design and locate offices, apartments, factories, highways and airports. They can eliminate the problem if consumers are willing to pay for it. Despite the fact that there appears to be some consumer demand for quiet products, legislation to control noise is wanting. Thus far, either widespread public pressure for strong anti-noise laws is lacking or is not yet being expressed.

In the final analysis, the most important weapon in the fight against noise is public awareness. One of the most successful groups advocating city quiet is New York City's Citizens for a Quieter City. Robert Baron, the group's founder, has been making people aware of the possibilities of noise control for several years. Another group, NOISE (National Organization to Insure Sound-Controlled Environment), has banded together municipalities, civic organizations and other groups to curb the increasing pollution of the environment by sound, especially that caused by low-flying jet airplanes.

Under the right circumstances individuals can take matters into their own hands by instituting lawsuits. Noise pollution cases have been before the courts on occasion for many years, although only a handful have been won. However, court decisions have been rendered against automobile wrecking yards and an industrial plant for being nuisances because of excessive noise. Another court found a telephone company liable for personal injuries resulting from excessive sounds over the telephone. In New York, traffic noise was considered damaging to property in a highway right-of-way condemnation case. Decisions have been rendered against airlines for failure to adequately protect workers from the extreme sounds of the jet engines.

Noise, to a great extent, can be eliminated and our environment made more peaceful. To do it requires time and money, and most businesses as well as government agencies are unlikely to spend much of either one until they are made aware of the benefits of constructive action. Expenditures will be made when it becomes apparent to everyone that reduced noise levels will result not only in a happier environment, but a more productive one as well.

# Resource Management: Can We Achieve It?

## Section 3

*Our environment is a resource, and control of pollution is a part of resource management. If we are willing to pay the necessary costs associated with pollution controls, then progress is possible. However, we must remember that wise resource management may not be possible if the number of people on the earth continues to increase at the rate recorded during the past few decades.* Burton's paper Popullution *explores this problem and its implications for Canadians.*

*It is necessary for the success of a pollution control program that the various levels of government in Canada co-operate more closely. Clear areas of responsibility need to be established so that each level of government has the duty and the authority to regulate resource management within a specific region. At present parochial attitudes that exist between governmental levels cause conflict and contradiction within the sphere of pollution control.*

*Quite possibly, new forms of taxation need to be created to offset the cost of disposing of goods that are no longer wanted by the original purchaser. Industry also can be persuaded to restore or maintain the standards of the environment in areas affected by their operations by the use of various incentives. One such example now exists in the Sudbury area where crops are being grown on mine wastes.*

*Very basic questions still remain. Do Canadians want to embark on a program of true resource management? Do they want to maintain the natural environment? Are they prepared to accept some inconvenience to do so? If so, what can the individual do to help achieve progress? The last article in the book,* What You Can Do, *makes certain positive suggestions. Will you respond to the challenge?*

# Popullution

## or

# Notes on the Coming Spaceship Society

**Ian Burton**

An unforeseen consequence of the human exploration of space has been its effect upon our thinking about the earth. All the money spent on the space program has probably been worth those spectacular photographs of the earth from space, or of the earthrise over the moon's horizon, and the drama of men on a damaged spacecraft struggling to get back to earth. Worth it because we have now all seen and realized in a way that has caught the popular imagination that the earth itself is a spaceship and that mankind is the crew.

There are some startling facts about the spaceship earth when you look at it in this new light. The size of the crew is increasing very rapidly. Not because more men are needed to man the spaceship – far from it. But because they have found no way of controlling their number and cannot even agree among themselves that it is desirable to do so. At last count there were about 3.5 billion crew members. In the next thirty years they *plan* to double that number to about 7.0 billion. *Plan* is really the wrong word because they haven't decided that they want 7.0 billion crew members. It's just that they know that's what will happen if things continue the way they are going. And everybody seems to agree that there's no likely way of stopping it, at least not in the next thirty years.

Also the spaceship earth has no pilot and no captain. The crew is divided into warring and distrustful factions. Each faction has its leaders but none can agree on how to achieve an acceptable leadership or a captain for the whole spaceship.

Another alarming thing about the spaceship earth is that the crew are using up and destroying their life support systems at a fast rate.

There is no doubt that the spaceship earth is in serious danger and its whole crew, however large, may be wiped out as a result of their own foolishness and cupidity. One promising sign is that some members of the crew, including some of the most powerful and influential members, are now becoming alive to the situation. They do not fully understand the dimensions of their problem, but at least they now begin to see dimly a new image of themselves and their spaceship.

Part of this new perception is the realization that the growing population, the lack of a recognizable world government, and the warring nations, are related to the great inequalities of wealth among different groups of the population and the destruction of life support systems by pollution. It is often stated that "pollution is a people problem" or that "to live is to pollute." Are these assertions valid and what do they portend? Or what is popullution?

## Pollution in the Global Village

Certainly pollution is partly a function of the size and density of population. The old-timers used to say that "a running stream purifies itself every ten miles." This statement was not totally false in a society where population was sparse. But where concentrations of people are high the quantity of waste materials becomes too high for the environment to absorb and dissipate. So more people does mean more pollution.

Does this have to be so? Is pollution inevitable? A certain amount of environmental destruction and contamination is necessary for each human being. So one way to curtail pollution is to restrict population growth in one way or another. Some of us are coming to see this as the main problem. Let me remind you for a moment about the world population figures.

TABLE I

WORLD POPULATION

| | | YEARS TO ADD 1 BILLION |
|---|---|---|
| 1830 | 1 Billion | |
| 1930 | 2 Billion | 100 |
| 1960 | 3 Billion | 30 |
| 1970 | 3.5 Billion | 15 |
| 1975 | 4.0 Billion | |
| 2000 | 7.0 Billion | average of 8.3 |

It took the whole history and prehistory of our species up to about 1830 to produce a population of 1 billion humans. The second billion was added in the 100 years from 1830 to 1930. The third billion was added in 30 years from 1930 to 1960 with the great events of the depression and World War II making no noticeable impact on global population. We now have a population of about 3.5 billion and are well on our way to adding the fourth billion in the space of only fifteen years from 1960 to 1975. Beyond 1975 the prospects look worse, pointing to a probably world population in the order of 7 billion by the year 2000. At that time we will be adding a billion souls every five years or so.

How much pollution will those future astronomical populations produce? Each new person adds some pollution to the planet, but in this as in other things people are not the same. All people are equally polluters but some are a lot more equal than others. The amount of pollution we create is partly a function of total numbers, but it is much more a function of level of consumption. And consumption is very unequal.

Per capita use of steel in the United States is fifty times the level in India. The average American uses over 40 kilogrammes of newsprint a year. Canadians use only 27 kilogrammes. The average Indian uses 0.2 kilogrammes. The U.S. per capita use of newsprint is 209 times that of

*The mouth of the Don River, Toronto.*

India. Canada is 135 times that of India. For energy the picture is similar. Per capita use of energy in the U.S.A. is running about 57 times that of India. Canadian consumption of energy is running about 20% behind that of the U.S. on a per capita basis, but it is still 46 times the Indian level.

As we all know it is the massive and unprecedented level of consumption in North America that is having a dramatic effect upon our environment. There is not a perfect correlation between the level of consumption and impact upon environment. There is hope that new pollution control technology will reduce significantly our rate of environmental destruction. But while new technology may buy time it is not a way out. Developing the technology to reduce one kind of pollution usually seems to end up creating other sorts of pollution, or other unexpected side effects. As Gross National Product* rises so does the impact of a nation's economy upon its own environment, and not only its own environment. It is the industrial nations that are chiefly responsible for the modification of the earth's atmosphere. It is the industrial nations

* *Gross National Product* (GNP) is the value of all goods and services produced by a nation for a specified year.

that threaten to upset the ecological balance of the planet and it is the industrial nations which are destroying the environment of other countries, especially those from which they draw their industrial raw materials and to which they are exporting new technology in the form of insecticides, herbicides and fertilizers, all of which are desperately needed if the growing populations are to be provided with enough food and basic necessities of shelter and clothing. It is not possible to state the marginal rate of environmental pollution, but the chances are that for each new dollar added to gross global product the amount by which pollution increases gets a little larger. It is for good reasons that the economist's figure of G.N.P. has been falling into disrepute and is sardonically referred to as gross national pollution.

From my earlier figures about different consumption levels I infer that the environmental impact of a North American is about fifty times that of a person in a developing or a poor country. And as we know the gap is widening. We are now engaged in a massive but fictitious enterprise known as economic development for developing countries. These poor countries are struggling to raise their level of consumption. The model that their leaders have in mind, and that we have in mind for them, and the promise that is held out to the suffering masses is that one day they too can become an industrialized nation with high mass consumption like North America or Western Europe or even the Soviet Union. It's true that we caution them that it will take a long time. Lester Pearson's report for the World Bank called *Partners in Development* suggests for example that at the present rate of development it will take Indonesia about 400 years to get to where the U.S. is now. Nevertheless development on the western pattern is the model.

This has great significance in pollution terms. Just assuming for a brief moment that we could stop the population of the world growing now and arrest it at the present level of 3.5 billion, of that 3.5 billion only 34% or 1.2 billion were regarded as being in the developed world in the Pearson Report. That is to say that 2.3 billion people now live in developing or poor countries. Let's be conservative and say only 2.0 billion. If each of these two billion people were to attain a North American level of consumption it would be the equivalent in environmental degradation terms at present standards of technology of fifty times that number, or approximately 100 billion. In other words with only today's world population and no more people at all, but given the consumption levels which we are enjoying it would be the same as having the equivalent of 100 billion people in the developing countries.

Ecologists seriously doubt that the world can support another 100 million North Americans with rapidly rising levels of consumption in the next thirty years, but the notion of bringing the rest of the world to our standards is frightening. And all this is on the assumption of a stable population now, discounting that probable doubling of world population by the year 2000. Let us not become too obsessed with the idea of doubling the world's population by the year 2000, but let us also recognize that the problems of social and economic justice in the global village are themselves of even greater significance.

What does this portend? What does it mean? It means to me that economic development for developing countries in the terms we now discuss it is simply a hoax being perpetrated on the population of poor countries by the rich countries and as often as not by the leaders of the poor countries themselves. It means that the population and pollution problem is not just a question of numbers but of standard of living. It means that adding one Canadian to the world's population is as serious as adding 50 Indians or Africans or Chinese. It means that population is a problem for the rich countries too, perhaps even more than for the poor countries.

We have tended to regard the population problem as something to be worried about by India and China and countries in South America but not by ourselves. The Pearson Report makes thirteen recommendations on population. The kind of advice given to the poor countries is as follows:

> Developing countries should identify their population problems
> if they have not already done so, recognize the relevance of
> population growth to their social and economic planning, and
> adopt appropriate programs. (p. 206)

This is rather a cautious admonition and says nothing about population control out of deference to some of their sensibilities although that is clearly what is meant. The population problem in developed countries is not recognized at all, no doubt out of deference to our much greater sensibilities. One not unfairly selected recommendation reads:

> Developed countries should initiate or strengthen their own
> facilities for population studies.

In other words the rich countries that are doing most of the damage to the life support systems on the spaceship earth had better study the population problem some more while the poor countries get down to controlling their population size. Small wonder that some politicians in developing countries read racist undertones into *our* concern about their population problems. And it is no surprise that the leaders of the developing countries do not take the environmental pollution problem very seriously. In their view it is hypocritical for the rich industrial nations to try to impress them with the need for sound environmental quality management. They are more inclined to assert their rights to do their own share of polluting the planet.

From a global perspective, looking at the spaceship earth there seems to be a strong case for limiting or trying to limit population, both in the developing countries and in the rich industrial nations. If we take our own population problem seriously then the developing countries are more likely to do the same.

*Making the Canadian Scene*

Now I turn to examine the population and pollution problem in Canada. It has long been our assumption that Canada is a big empty land and that more people are needed to develop its resources and build up the country. Talking in 1967 to the Royal Society of Canada about our future water needs and the reasons why we should not export water to the United States, the late General A. G. L. McNaughton said, "Canada has been endowed by Divine Providence with abundant resources which confer immense advantages upon this country. It is our responsibility to use these resources with discretion, and to treasure the more basic of them for the generations of Canadian citizens who will come after us . . . The northward course of our Prairie empire is already being staked out by prospectors . . ." We are now beginning to doubt the wisdom of our expansionist philosophy. It does not necessarily follow that Canada would be a better country if there were 100 million of us rather than 20 million. More people in Canada will probably mean more pollution here too. It will certainly mean bigger cities, more expressways cutting through downtown neighbourhoods, more dense high-rise living, more difficult access to open space and the countryside and so on. It is by no means obvious that bigger means better. Nor is it safe to assume that the faster the growth the better.

And yet we continue to strive to be bigger and to grow rapidly. As a nation we Canadians still do not give serious thought to population issues. We really have no national population policy except a mindless assumption that more will mean better. But think about it for a minute. A population of 40 million Canadians in the year 2000 would be heavily concentrated in a few major urban regions. Fully 8 million or 20% of the total would be in the Toronto-centered urban region. It is confidently predicted that the population of the present area of Metropolitan Toronto will grow to 5 million by the end of the century. As I contemplate that Toronto of the future I can imagine few aspects of life being better than they are now except for a privileged few. On the other hand I can readily see how the quality of life will be worse, for many people and in many ways. Some of the leaders of the business community can think of nothing better than building a New York or a Los Angeles or a Chicago in southern Ontario. I can think of few worse ideas.

What do we assume people are for? In former times large populations have seemed desirable to ensure the survival of the tribe, to make nations more powerful, to aggrandize the rulers, and as a supply of labor for production purposes. These reasons have now lost their force. More people may imperil our chances of survival, not improve them, modern weapons of mass destruction are making huge armies obsolete and Trudeaumania notwithstanding we really don't need more people for that purpose. Automation and methods of mass production are displacing the need for more people as producers. Trade unions are forced to adopt restrictive practices to safeguard the jobs of their members, and at a time of strong inflationary pressures we have a totally unacceptable rate of unemployment.

There is a prevailing myth which does explain some of our views about population. This is the idea that more population means expanding markets and expanding profits and more jobs and more tax revenues. Listen for a moment to the words of Maurice C. R. Taylor, Senior Vice-President of the Greenwin Development group. In the Toronto *Star* for 12th May 1970 he wrote:

> A city is not just a collection of roads and buildings. It is a
> vast business enterprise, managed by elected and appointed
> officials for the benefit of its citizens. Good management requires
> good planning, and municipal and provincial authorities have
> prepared, in conjunction with planning experts and consultants
> from all over the world, official plans for the development of
> Toronto and the surrounding boroughs. These plans set forth
> guidelines for the future growth of the entire area, establishing,
> among other things, large sections within the city and its
> suburbs especially for high-rise apartment development.
> These official plans recognize the enormous future need for

multiple and high-rise units to house the ever-increasing population of what has become North America's fastest growing city.

Who says the population should be ever increasing? Obviously such a prospect looks good for the Greenwins of the world. And the majority of people are still persuaded that it is good for them too. I suspect that if you took a poll of the citizens today they would agree with Mr. Taylor. Expansion is good for us, it means more tax revenues for the city and more jobs. But I also think that substantially more people than five years ago are now ready to question this philosophy. More people are wondering why when the city keeps growing and developing and getting more tax revenue that there are not enough jobs, and the taxes on the ordinary man in the street still go up and up, and there is inflation and the quality of life in some respects gets worse.

*Pollution in the Just Society*

Beyond the reasons of profit motive and pride and ambition for power lies a more serious social concern. We are becoming increasingly intolerant and impatient with the social injustices that exist in our own society. If the size of the national cake is expanding strongly then the poor and the underprivileged can be persuaded to wait and have patience. "Do not demand justice now, but in the interests of the whole society stop rocking the boat and we promise to improve your lot very soon." As the size of the cake grows even the smallest slice gets bigger. If we have a more stable society with no population growth and slow growth in further consumption then demands for social justice will be insistent and immediate and potentially explosive. Robert Stanfield is not a man that I am accustomed to quoting. Recently he said:

> No program of social justice can be satisfied unless there is a sound and expanding economic base to support it.

Mr. Stanfield! Social justice has nothing to do with expansion. It has to do with equal opportunity, and equitable laws, and fair taxation systems, and access to education, and legal redress. Expansion has only to do with telling the underprivileged and those who have less than justice to wait a bit and be patient.

If this holds true on a national scale between people and class groups it also holds true on a global scale. If we are not to overload the spaceship earth and destroy our life support systems we must curb population growth in all countries and control and drastically alter the patterns of consumption in the industrial nations. Not to face up to this problem could well mean suicide for us all. But if we do try to face up to it we cannot hope to do so without generating much political turmoil, and without drastically changing our own attitudes and beliefs. A stabilized world population can probably only be brought about by a world authority. We have got to get a mission control for the spaceship earth. Only in that way can we hope to achieve social and economic justice on a global scale. It is no use relying on appeals to the conscience of the rich nations to come to the aid of the poor. That only produces a system in which the poor people in rich countries are taxed to give help to the rich people in poor countries! Social justice cannot be achieved by appeals to conscience in Canada and anywhere else. As members of the C.L.C. well understand, guidelines or "moral suasion" whether set at 6% or 10% or any number, can only result in some complying or being more or less obliged to comply while others do not. This can only create more distrust and social tension. In the prevailing climate of the times socially desirable goals can be sought by providing incentives for desirable behavior or penalties for undesirable behavior or by a variety of forms of coercive regulation and legislation with appropriate penalties for infractions. This applies to wages and prices as it also applies to polluters, and will eventually have to apply also to breeding.

Attempts to achieve a just society in a world of expanding population inevitably lead to curtailment of individual freedoms. This is the dilemma (or as Garrett Hardin calls it, "the tragedy") of public goods or common property resources. The things that belong to everybody belong to nobody and lack of rights leads to lack of responsibilities. The history of western society can be viewed as a process of narrowing individual liberty for the common good as population increases. At an earlier time it was not necessary to have complete private ownership of land. Much land in mediaeval villages, for example, was owned in common. All or most people in the village community had the right to graze their cattle on the commons. The system is not stable over time and breaks down because it is to the advantage of each farmer to add more cattle to his own herd even to and beyond the point at which the land becomes overgrazed and the soil eroded. For the individual the rational decision is to add another cow. He gets all or nearly all the value of the additional cow and the loss in quality of grazing land is shared by the whole community. A rational policy for the individual is suicidal for the society. To overcome this problem private ownership of land has become the chosen solution. That, of course, is not the only way, but all solutions involve the curtailment of individual freedom to use the land, which is the common heritage of us all.

Curtailment of the freedom to use land in the way an individual wishes has preceded similar curtailment of the use of air and water. Air and water have traditionally been regarded as free goods available to anyone to enjoy and to do with whatever he pleased. But as our population has grown and levels of industrial production and consumption have risen and as people have become more concentrated in urban areas, we are now realizing that we must curtail the freedom to dump your industrial and municipal wastes into rivers and lakes. And we must curtail the right to burn your wastes and put them into the atmosphere. These losses of freedom come as the inevitable result of the growth of population and the development of industry and they affect each and every one of us. For a while we were satisfied by appeals to conscience. The Ontario Water Resources Commission went around politely asking people not to pollute. But it didn't do much good except to prepare the way for the day when we really have to get tough with those polluters.

The same will be true of population. Appeals are now beginning to be made that you should not have more than two children. I have suggested as much myself at a pollution conference in Windsor last March. Now I am convinced that the value of such appeals is only that they will help to prepare for the day when regulations are necessary.

Of course, I recognize that this flies in the face of conventional wisdom and accepted social attitudes. In 1967 some thirty nations passed the following resolution at the U.N.:

> The Universal Declaration of Human Rights describes the
> family as the natural and fundamental unit of society. It follows
> that any choice and decision with regard to the size of the
> family must irrevocably rest with the family itself and cannot
> be made by anybody else.

To introduce coercion into the limitation of the family size is going to require a tremendous revolution of attitudes. But perhaps not much more so than was required to curtail access to land and to free use of air and water. To us it seems incredible that at one time people could add as many cattle to the herd that grazed upon the land that was held in common with others in the community. It is fast becoming unbelievable that only a few years ago people could discharge effluent freely into the waters and the atmosphere. If civilized society survives in Canada for a second hundred years until 2067 I predict that they will be saying, "Goodness, can you imagine, in the 20th century people could have as many children as they felt like having and nobody took steps to prevent them. In fact they even had social policies to encourage larger family sizes."

When George Orwell wrote in 1949 a book called *1984* he envisaged a brave new world that all found repugnant. It is quite possible that the world I have been forecasting will have some of the features of 1984. When I read Orwell way back in my schooldays I was not particularly alarmed because I could not imagine why anybody would really want to help create such a society. But then I didn't know about the spaceship earth. Now I find myself contemplating Huxley or Orwellian solutions with less than total horror or at any rate arguing that if we do not eventually curtail the freedom to breed then the journey of our spaceship will end in disaster. That is the meaning of 'popullution'.

# Many Lives Are Being Saved as London Beats Pollution

LONDON – When the polar bears began to grow whiter in London's Regent Park Zoo, it was plain to almost everyone that something strange was occurring.

Colors everywhere were brighter, in nature and in the fabrics people wore.

Home gardeners boasted of astonishing successes with varieties of flowers they had feared to tackle. Roses bloomed where none had ever appeared in human memory. In the square mile of London's City, the financial heart of the country, some quarter of a million plants of various kinds flourished and in built-up areas of the sprawling metropolis swifts and house martins reappeared and sometimes nested.

The reason, like the air, seems clear: London is winning its battle against pollution.

*Haze Gone*

Custodians of some of the city's major architectural treasures were among the first to react to the altering circumstances. St. Paul's Cathedral has been cleaned, and results are spectacular. The haze that often shrouded its looming majesty has disappeared. In the clear light of a wintry morning, it glows now like rich old ivory.

Nelson's Column and the National Gallery in Trafalgar Square have a new beauty. As the grime is stripped from Albert Hall its patrons, young and old, are discovering an unknown vitality in the Victorian mosaics of its exterior. A similar face-lifting is planned for the Houses of Parliament.

The change can be measured in other than subjective and esthetic terms. London has 53 hours more of winter sunshine than it had a decade ago and 122 hours more in the whole year. An unknown but considerable number of people are alive who might otherwise have died.

Nor is the transformation limited to London alone. Manchester and Leeds have hopes of spring flowers. Market garden yields are improving. On bright days people can eat lunch outdoors in Glasgow's George Square without any overlay of grit.

*Black Areas*

Some 42 per cent of the acreage and 52 per cent of the dwellings in the so-called "black areas" of the country are now included in "smokeless zones." This doesn't mean that the smoke nuisance has been conquered entirely; still less that such insidious pollutants as sulphur dioxide have been banished. But London's smoke reading, for example, is only about one-fifth of what it was.

# Pollution Attack Delayed by 'Parochial Attitudes'

**Basil Jackson**

The lines in the behind-the-scene legislative battle for pollution control in Canada are becoming clearer.

First public disclosure of the different viewpoints of the provinces vis-à-vis Ottawa came recently when the federal government made a policy statement on the Canada Water Act to be introduced into the Commons this fall (FP, June 28).

Ontario – and more specifically the Ontario Water Resources Commission – reacted initially against federal intervention in administrative control of water pollution within the province.

(The British North America Act of 1867 makes water and air pollution a provincial responsibility.)

Now it appears that Ottawa – however delicately it approaches the provinces to try to get some degree of uniformity and nationwide action in anti-pollution measures – faces some parochial attitudes.

Many provinces rightly or wrongly believed Ottawa's action would usurp their own rights under the BNA Act. This attitude – at least in Ontario – is beginning to die.

On the other hand, the provinces would no doubt be pleased to have financial help from Ottawa to allow them to fight pollution on their own terms, or at least do some basic research for them.

The initial concern of Ontario about federal intervention into the province's water pollution problems was later mollified by George Kerr, Ontario's Minister of Energy Resources Management (responsible for pollution control) after meeting Otto Lang, federal minister responsible for energy and water policy.

"We welcome Ottawa's entry. The fact that all provinces would be covered by pollution control legislation will make our job easier.

"We won't face possible loss of industries from our pollution penalties," Kerr said.

Kerr's reference to industry touches a tender spot with all provincial premiers and ministers responsible for attracting new industries to their province.

# Using Vegetation to Stabilize Mine Tailings

**T. H. Peters**

Stabilization of mine tailings has concerned the mining industry for years. Efficient metallurgical processes now enable the development of low-grade ore bodies containing as little as one per cent metals. The result is an increase in waste materials that must be eliminated.

In 1968 total ore production from the International Nickel Company's mines in Ontario rose to a record of 24,350,000 dry short tons. To achieve this record and the subsequent extraction of the metals contained in the ore involves the largest mining complex of its kind in the world. The company's Ontario division presently operates nine mines, one open pit, four concentrators, two smelters, an iron ore recovery plant, a copper refinery near Sudbury, and a nickel refinery at Port Colborne.

The waste products of the concentrators are "tailings," which are barren rock particles removed from the ore through a system of crushing, pulverizing, and flotation. Some tailings are returned underground for use as mine fill. The remainder are mixed with water and pumped out as slurry through large-diameter pipe lines to disposal areas.

Tailings have the texture of fine beach sand. They are composed mainly of silica, with some iron, calcium, magnesium, etc. About 50,000 tons of tailings are produced daily by International Nickel's four concentrators in Ontario.

About 30 years ago the company began experimenting with ways to stabilize the surface of tailings of the Copper Cliff concentrator and thus prevent them from becoming a source of dust under certain weather conditions. Using chemicals to form seals, covering with crushed limestone, mulching with straw, and attempting to establish vegetation were among the methods tried. Results were either unsuccessful or economically impractical.

The first significant breakthrough came in the spring of 1957. An attempt to establish vegetation on three test plots produced success on one plot. In fact, the same basic procedures used on that plot are still used today.

The experiments with vegetation establishment continued through 1960 when test plots reached an individual size of two acres. A review of experimental procedures in 1960 indicated that successful establishment depended on three practices:

1. Seedings should first be made in a location as close as possible to the windward edge of the tailings area. This eliminates the blasting and burying of the young seedlings by drifting tailings.

2. A companion or nurse crop should be used to provide shade and reduce surface wind, and snow fencing should be erected in exposed areas to reduce wind velocity.

3. Sufficient plant nutrients should be supplied and made available by supplying limestone sufficiently in advance of seeding to permit the pH of the areas to approach the neutral zone.

An additional factor determining the success of a seeding became apparent as larger acreages were planted. That was time of planting. Seedings in August which generally germinated under cooler temperatures and with more available moisture were consistently more successful. Young plants from seedings in late May or early June invariably struggled during the hot, dry conditions of July and frequently died.

In 1961 the first large block of tailings – 100 acres – was seeded. Since then, the annual acreage seeded has ranged from 50 to 120 acres and now totals over 600 acres.

Readily available agricultural equipment was used at all times in the seeding program with one exception. Hydroseeding equipment, using a paper pulp mulch, was used on one exposed area to ensure germination.

A gradual evolution in types and quantities of fertilizer used has occurred, but the program followed today is much the same as the first one devised in 1957.

Early in June, feed-grade limestone is applied at the rate of three tons per acre and disced into the soil. Feed-grade limestone is slightly coarser than agricultural limestone and therefore breaks down more slowly, providing a longer pH buffering period.

About July 10, additional limestone is applied at the rate of two tons per acre. This is immediately followed with an application of 5-20-20 fertilizer at the rate of 400 pounds per acre. Then the ground is harrowed. High analysis fertilizer is used to provide plant nutrients at the lowest possible cost per unit.

Seeding begins about the third week of July. A conventional farm seed drill is used. Seeding is accompanied by another application of 5-20-20 fertilizer at the rate of 300 pounds per acre. Fall rye harvested from the last year's seeding is sown as a companion crop at the rate of 1½ bushels per acre. The grass seed mixture consists of 12½ pounds of Canada bluegrass and 12½ pounds of mixed seed containing 1 part timothy, 2 parts red top, 1 part Kentucky bluegrass, 1 part crested wheatgrass, and 1 part creeping red fescue.

Immediately after this seeding, Bromegrass is seeded with an Alvan Blanch seeder at the rate of 10 pounds per acre. A cultipacker is then used to firm the seedbed. Germination generally occurs in about 10 days.

Once the grass is established, an annual maintenance program is carried out. Two hundred pounds of 5-20-20 fertilizer per acre is applied immediately after cutting. In late fall, after freeze-up, urea is spread at the rate of 100 pounds per acre. On longer-established areas, both fertilizer and lime are applied on the basis of chemical tests indicating nutrient deficiencies.

Some grass is cut and marketed as hay for livestock. Sales have reached several thousand bales in recent years. Trees, principally birch, are voluntarily growing from seed throughout the area. Some have reached a height of 4 feet.

Although grass has been established on well over 600 acres, experiments are continuing in an effort to find improved practices. Current work focuses on higher-analysis fertilizers, the lowering of competition between the companion crop and grass seedlings, and the establishment of legumes.

# Beautify Canada —
# Or Not?

**Basil Jackson**

Pollution is a nine-letter dirty word guaranteed to raise emotions to white-hot levels.

The world of pollution is divided into two camps – "them" and "us". That is, the pollutors and the polluted.

The pollutors are:

– Primary industry such as mining, pulp and paper, steelmaking, oil refining and the petro-chemical industries. All these industries pollute surrounding waters and air.

– Secondary industry: food processing plants, metalplating factories, tanneries, metal fabricating plants such as car factories, and other manufacturing plants producing industrial wastes. These operations are liable to pollute water resources.

– Cities, towns and villages which discharge raw human ordure into rivers, lakes and streams. Also, municipalities which build primary sewage treatment plants and defer installing secondary treatment equipment.

– Transportation systems that use fossil fuels for powering prime movers. Motor vehicles, airplanes – especially jets – pollute the air. Ships and boats pollute both water and air.

The polluted are the people of Canada who breathe the invisible but smelly sulphur dioxide and carbon monoxide gases in cities; the child who turns away from the old swimming hole because it it now fouled with scummy algae; the fisherman who watches dead fish float belly-up on a once-sparkling lake.

But the polluted, while they blame "them" – and the government – for letting them get away with pollution, rarely think about their own contribution to pollution.

How many of us:

– Think about the sulphur dioxide and other gases emitted from the chimneys of our spanking new suburban bungalows?

– Check to see if the PCV (pressure control valve costing $2 to $3) of our car's anti-pollution system is working?

– Carelessly toss litter out of the car window?

What are the unemotional facts about pollution control in Canada today?

Several provincial governments – but not enough – are putting increasing pressure on industry and municipalities to clean up; in general, industry and local authorities are cooperating; and the polluted – you and I – are paying the shot, either through increased taxes or by paying more for a product.

As one industrial manager put it: "We spend millions of dollars on anti-pollution equipment and we don't get a cent out of it. What we spend on pollution control we tack on to the end price of the products we make."

Is it working?

Yes – but slowly. Basically, it depends on how much money the taxpayer is willing to pay to combat pollution.

"Society has to decide if it will pay the cost," says Dr. E. A. Watkinson, director general, Health Services Branch, Department of National Health & Welfare, Ottawa.

"Technological breakthroughs are going to be essential, too. As for the cash – we're optimistic that it will be forthcoming," he said, looking through his 11th story window at the magnificent Ottawa River – polluted with raw sewage from the city of Hull, on the opposite bank, by Ottawa's own primary treatment effluent, and by pulp and paper mills and municipalities further upstream.

It all depends on how fast industry – on the Great Lakes shoreline in particular – pours more money into anti-pollution measures and curtails the amount of acids, phenols, phosphates and poisons being discharged into this biggest of all North American water resources.

Are we winning the battle of the Great Lakes?

"We are not winning it," says A. D. P. Heeney, chairman of the Canadian section of International Joint Commission, Ottawa. "The waters are still deteriorating in Lake Erie and in Lake Ontario, for example."

"But there are prospects of reversing the deterioration," Heeney believes. "We understand the problems better now, although there are still some scientific mysteries – such as what goes on in the process called eutrophication."

One of the reasons for the clearer understanding of the problems in combatting water pollution is the stronger stand Ottawa is taking to coordinate these efforts.

Unfortunately, owing to the inhibitions of the British North America Act, pollution is a provincial responsibility despite the fact that air and water pollution disregard not only provincial borders, but even international frontiers.

Despite this problem the government is slowly developing a tough attitude. It is determined to halt pollution, and is giving a lead to the provinces.

Some moves so far:
– The establishment of the Inland Waters Branch of the Department of Energy, Mines & Resources. It is now building the $23.5-million Canada Centre for Inland Waters, at Burlington, Ont. It will be a research centre to tackle Great Lakes pollution problems – and eventually all of Canada's inland water problems.

The branch is setting up 357 water-sampling stations across Canada to collect hitherto unavailable data on water resources. These data will be given to the provinces and correlated with the province's own information.

Ottawa is hammering out a Canada Water Act expected to be tabled in the House of Commons this autumn.

"It will define in some measure Ottawa's responsibility for water quality," says Dr. A. T. Prince, director of the Inland Waters Branch.

"Anti-pollution science is an evolutionary rather than a revolutionary process," says Dr. J. L. Sullivan, head, Air Pollution Control Unit, Department of National Health & Welfare, Ottawa.

"We're standing still, from the principle viewpoint. We're using anti-pollution equipment today which operates on the same principle devised 30 years ago. Mind you, their efficiency has been much improved. It is much more sophisticated equipment now."

The principles he refers to – for air pollution control – are filtration, dynamic collectors, electrostatic precipitators, and air scrubbers. (In sewage treatment it is much the same story – no revolutionary breakthroughs.)

He believes one answer to reducing household chimney pollution is for more people to live in apartments. Instead of say 100 chimneys – if 100 families lived in separate houses – there would be one, and the apartment furnace would be fitted with anti-pollution equipment.

Dr. Sullivan's unit is coordinating air pollution research and control methods between the provinces and helping directly where it can.

In the works: a federal Clean Air Act which can be taken as a model by the provinces. So far there are no indications on what form the act will take. However, it seems definite that it will establish uniform standards of emissions from factory chimneys and also lay down standards for motor vehicle exhaust pollution.

Although Canadian inland waters – and some offshore waters – are heavily polluted in some places, the air in our cities is not – so far – as dirty as it is in London, New York, Brussels or Tokyo.

In Tokyo, policemen can only take a short spell at traffic duty because of the lack of oxygen in the air at some busy intersections. Before they go on duty they take a whiff of oxygen from a cylinder provided by the police department. Seventeen tons of dirt per square mile per month fall on the city.

Montreal and Toronto, our two most industrialized cities, are clean in comparison, although polluted.

However, Sudbury is an example of what can happen when smelting pollutes the atmosphere. The city and much of the surrounding district were frequently "gassed" with fumes. Now, under the aegis of the Ontario Pollution Control Act, administered by the Ontario Department of Health, the mining companies are beginning to clean up in earnest (FP, Dec. 7, 1968).

Ontario is a good example for the other provinces to follow. Before the province took over air pollution control from the 600-odd municipalities Jan. 1, 1968, very little was done to clean up.

Air pollution got into civic politics. The politicians – including those in Toronto – were frightened of passing anti-pollution measures for fear of driving industry away.

Since the takeover by the provincial government, air pollution control means what it says. The law has sharp teeth. It can cost an offender $2,000 for a smoking chimney – $5,000 if it's a corporation, plus $10,000 for each subsequent conviction.

In other words, if your company has a chimney that pours out offensive smoke, it could cost you $10,000 per day for as long as it smokes.

Recently the Ontario government announced that next year it will regulate development of gravel pits and limestone quarries in the southern part of the province in an effort to stop further "eye pollution."

Mines Minister Allan Lawrence says the province has to take control of these pits and quarries away from the municipalities.

"They just haven't been doing the job," he says.

Another recent and significant move by highly industrialized Ontario was the appointment of George Kerr as minister of Energy & Resources. He has been charged with taking an even tougher look at the pollution problems of the province.

An earlier move was the appointment of Donald J. Collins as chairman of the Ontario Water Resources Commission. His first major effort may be to hone the legal teeth now menacing water pollutors to an even finer sharpness. In the cards: a possibility of increasing the penalties for illegal waste disposal.

Labor unions are prime movers in battling industrial pollution if only to help improve working conditions in factories and living conditions near them.

There are numerous companies in Canada producing or supplying air and water pollution equipment and devices. It is almost impossible to establish how much business is conducted in this field.

At a rough estimate, the anti-pollution industry is worth about $70 million a year. This includes the whole gamut – from sewage treatment plants and structures to air filtration equipment.

The approved loans to municipalities by Central Mortgage & Housing Corp., Ottawa, to municipalities to build sewage treatment plants amounted to $35 million in 1968. It has run from a high of $43.3 million in 1962 to a low of $26.1 million in 1964.

# Pollution:
# What You Can Do

## Holly Santa-Barbara

Now that people are becoming increasingly concerned about our rapidly deteriorating environment, many are asking what they can do to help control pollution.

A lot of people still believe that the amount of pollution caused by one person is negligible, in terms of the over-all problem. Not so. For example, every person contributes about five pounds of garbage every day, and 826 pounds of algae (through phosphates in human sewage and detergents) to our lakes and rivers every year. As you can see, the problem is not only one of government and big industry, but of individual responsibility as well. Listed below are a few things each of us can do to ease the burden on our environment.

1. Detergents are a main source of pollution because of their high phosphate content. Use soap powders instead. Try adding a tablespoon or two of washing soda or bleach to soap powders. The results are remarkably similar and almost as effective as the heavy-duty high-phosphate detergents. Avoid water softeners and cleansing powders. Try more elbow grease and learn to live with hard water. Medical research has shown a lower incidence of cardiac disease in areas with hard water.

2. Use only white toilet paper, facial tissues and paper towels. The dyes used to colour these products, although pretty, are water pollutants.

3. Most aerosol sprays are air pollutants. If you must kill insects, try drowning them in water instead of in insecticide. Water works as well, but is not lethal to animal or plant life. Air fresheners, deodorants, etc., are all air pollutants too.

4. Don't throw away coat hangers you cannot use. Return them to the dry cleaners, if possible.

5. Avoid using non-returnable glass bottles and tin cans, as much as possible. These things don't decompose, and only add to the growing mountain of waste materials. Similarly, avoid using Styrofoam and plastic containers. When burned, these materials release highly poisonous gases.

6. Use your garbage can for things like cooking fats, coffee grounds, tea leaves – when these are flushed down the toilet, they clog drains and pollute water systems.

7. If you live in a rural area, save vegetable waste in a compost heap for use as a fertilizer.

8. Never leave water running unnecessarily. Turn the tap off when you are through. Our water supplies are far from unlimited.

9. Remember that both gas and electric power are two main sources of air pollution. If you are about to install a home heating system, think seriously of using natural gas. And use as few unnecessary electrical gadgets as possible. Try living without that electric knife, can opener, hair curling set, if you can. Strike up a conversation with your neighbour, husband, wife or kids instead of watching television in the evening. And turn off the lights when you leave a room.

10. Don't use disposable diapers unless you have to. Not only do they clog toilets, but they are also more expensive than cloth diapers in the long run.

11. When you shop, bring along your own shopping bags, and use them as often as possible. Unnecessary packaging is one of the biggest waste problems today. Don't let the supermarket load you down with piles of bags and wrappings – tell them you don't need them.

12. Don't flush filter-tip cigarettes down the toilet – they don't decompose either. Better still, don't smoke. Everyone who smokes carries around his own personal pollution problem, and fouls the air for everyone around him.

13. Don't light your fireplace or burn leaves. If you must light your fireplace, burn wood instead of coal.

14. Investigate the possibility of using natural botanical fertilizers for your garden in place of the usual phosphate-laden fertilizers.

15. Support your local public transportation system. If you must use your car, try to form a car pool, to minimize the number of automobiles on the road. Cars contribute half of all the air pollution in North America.

16. If you see a blatant example of air pollution (industry, public utilities, buildings, etc.) contact air pollution control authorities. They are most helpful, and will investigate any complaint you may have. Remember that the more people show concern, the more likely action will be taken.

17. Educate your friends, relatives and especially children about ways to stop pollution. Impress upon them the delicate balance of our environment, and tell them about specific things they can do to help.

18. Most important – if you do not have any children, consider seriously the possibility of limiting the number of children in your family to no more than two. If you decide you want more, adopt. After all, it's people who pollute, and the more people, the more pollution. Not only our lives, but the lives of our children and their children are what's at stake.

# Acknowledgem

The Publishers thank the following sources for permission to reprint material.

The Bureau of Outdoor Recreation, Mid-Continent Region, for **The Deafening Din**. (*The Balance*, April 14, 1970.)

Ian Burton, for **Popullution** or **Notes on the Coming Spaceship Society**. (This paper was originally presented to the 11th Farmer, Labor, Teacher Conference at Port Elgin, June 1970. The Conference was sponsored by the Ontario Federation of Labour in cooperation with the Canadian Labour Congress.)

The Canadian Press, for **Air Pollution 'Causes Most Human Diseases', There's Fishing in the Thames Again**.

Paul R. Ehrlich and the Editors of *Ramparts*, for **Eco-catastrophe**.

Nick Fillmore, for **Pollution Hitting the Hothouse?**

The *Financial Post*, for **Polluters or Not? It Depends on the Fuel, Ten-year Pollution Cleanup May Cost $5,000 Million, Pollution Attack Delayed by 'Parochial Attitudes', Beautify Canada – Or Not?**

The *Financial Times*, for **A New and Cheap Way of Treating Wastes**.

*Fortune*, for **We Can Afford Clean Air**. (Edmund K. Faltermayer is a member of *Fortune*'s Board of Directors. Reprinted from the November 1965 issue of *Fortune* magazine by special permission; © 1965 Time Inc.)

The *Geographical Review*, for **Geographical Aspects of Air Pollution**. (Reprinted with omissions from *Geographical Review*, Vol. 56, 1966; © the American Geographical Society of New York.)

The *Globe and Mail*, for **Only Pressure Will Do It, 10% of Cottages Pollute Lakes**.

H. B. N. Hynes, for **Why Lakes Become Green and Slimy**.

The *Journal of Soil and Water Conservation*, for **Using Vegetation to Stabilize Mine Tailings**. (Vol. 25, no. 2, March-April 1970.)

*Nation's Cities*, for **Wealth Out of Waste**. (*Nation's Cities*, September 1969, the magazine of the National League of Cities; © 1969.)

Southam News Services, for **Weedkiller Still Used Here**.

The *Spectator*, for **An Eerie Silence Settles Over Erie, 'Philosophy Change' Needed in Great Lakes Water Use, Scientists Can Start at Beginning in Fight Against Heat Pollution, Sophisticated Oil Pollution Detectors Coming, Mercury Spills in More Rivers, Dow Won't Compensate Fishermen, Polluters Are Thieves: Kerr, Private Phosphate Probe Follows Gov't 'Secret', Pitfalls in New Mining Plans, To DDT or Not to DDT, Pollution: What You Can Do**.

The *Times*, for **Mysterious Pollution: The Green Infection**.

The *Toronto Telegram*, for **Is a World that Makes Ecological Sense Only a Dream?, New Law Won't Halt Pollution – Prober, The Common Death of a Duck, Pesticide Pollution Could Be Cut in Half, Zoologist Says.**

The *Unesco Courier*, for **The Biosphere**.

United Press International, for **Oceans Pollution Seen Threat to Climate, Many Lives Are Being Saved as London Beats Pollution**.

Doug Wright, for cartoon on page 126.

**This book is to be returned on or before
the last date stamped below.**

2 5 APR 1997